KNOW THE SPIRIT

Know the Spirit

Rediscovering the Person and Power of the Holy Spirit

Rob Warner

VINE
BOOKS

Servant Publications
Ann Arbor, Michigan

Vine Books is an imprint of Servant Publications especially designed to
serve Evangelical Christians.

Published by Servant Books
P.O. Box 8617
Ann Arbor, Michigan 48107

Cover design by Michael Andaloro
Cover photograph by O.S. Henderson/The Image Bank

Printed in the United States of America
ISBN 0-89283-377-7

88   89   90   91   92   93   10   9   8   7   6   5   4   3   2   1

This work was first published in Great Britain by Hodder and Stoughton
Limited.

This book is dedicated to my wife,
Claire,
whose example teaches me more about
life in the Spirit every day.

This book would not have been possible
but for all we received from the fellowship of
St. Michael-le-Belfrey, York
1975–1979.

CONTENTS

FOREWORD

The Holy Spirit has been discovered and rediscovered by more and more people in the last fifty years. Book after book has been written and the subject has by no means been fully exhausted if for no other reason than that the subject itself is inexhaustible. Since the Holy Spirit is the third person of the Trinity and therefore is God, one can easily see that we will go on discovering more things about the Spirit as we search the Scriptures and find materials that escaped the eyes of commentators and students across the years.

From the historical perspective we should note how limited even the finest expressions of doctrinal statements can be. The Westminster Confession of Faith certainly is one of the greatest, if not the greatest, expression of the Reformed faith. Yet that Confession was shortsighted in its treatment of the Holy Spirit. This Confession was adopted in 1729 and almost two hundred years passed before it was amended to include a reasonably full statement about the Spirit. In 1902-1903 the Confession was amended to include not only a statement on the Holy Spirit but also one on "the love of God and missions." The latter had to do with another oversight on the part of the framers of the Confession, namely the obligation of the Church to preach the Gospel of Jesus Christ unto all the world and to make disciples of all nations.

It is with this in mind that we approach the work of Rob Warner in his excellent book which has for its objective a biblical study of the person and work of the Holy Spirit. The book is thoroughly biblical in its compass. It covers many aspects of the subject with which all of its readers will be in full agreement. But it goes beyond this for Mr. Warner skillfully deals with issues that are very controversial in today's world. I have in mind the gifts of the Holy Spirit and more particularly speaking in tongues and prophecy. But before discussing these matters it is important to note that this book is designed to do more than discuss the Holy Spirit didactically. The author is seriously interested in the subjective aspect of the Spirit's work, namely that Christians should experience the Spirit who in-dwells them and should grow and keep on growing in the Holy Spirit. He is strong in his emphasis that no one has gone as far as he or she can in growth in the Spirit. And all too many of us are only beginning to rediscover all of the blessings which are ours but which we have not yet come to know in our daily Christian walk.

The discussion of the gifts of the Spirit will be painful for those in the Christian community who hold that some of the Spirit's gifts have ceased to be available for all practical pur-poses and are not repeatable today. Indeed at times one is inclined to say that some believers are far more sure of what the Spirit does not, and cannot, do than they are of what he can do and does do in spite of that. Warner is seeking to make it clear that the Lord is in the heavens and he does what he pleases (Ps 115:3). And since the Holy Spirit is God, he does what he pleases and in doing so seems to be giving offense to a few. In the case of speaking in tongues, there are those who claim that this is demonic and not of God or the Spirit of God.

Warner is saying that he speaks in tongues and has found it helpful and useful to him in his spiritual journey. But if there can be no speaking in tongues, then his experience is false and his word of testimony turns out to be untruthful. I am quite unready to label speaking in tongues as false and impossible, even though I do not claim to have this gift. But this leads on to the question of prophecy, healing and the like. Arthur T. Pierson was a dear brother before his times who had discovered some things about the Spirit that others have not yet caught up on. In his delightful book *The New Acts of the Apostles,* published in 1894, he spoke about Hans Egede and his wife, missionaries to Greenland, of whom he said concerning the people of that region:

Those stupid dwarfs, like the icebergs and snowfields

xi

about them, seemed frozen into insensibility; and, feeling that only some sure sign of Divine power could melt their stolid apathy, Egede boldly asked for the gift of healing, and was permitted in scores of cases to exercise it, while his wife received the gift of prophecy, predicting in the crisis of famine the very day and hour when a ship should come bearing supplies (p. 84).

If this could and did happen in the late seventeenth and eighteenth centuries, it may be time for us to claim again gifts that lie dormant if for no other reason than Christians either do not believe these gifts are for today or they have failed to see the truth of the Bible and do not accept the witness of people who have experienced these gifts.

This brings me back full circle to the Westminster Confession of Faith. In the revision of that Confession in the realm of the work of the Holy Spirit the statement has this rather odd sentence: "The Holy Spirit, whom the Father is ever willing to give to all who ask Him. . . ." Since when did we have to ask for the Holy Spirit? Orthodox theology has always asserted that we are sealed and indwelt by the Holy Spirit from the moment we are born again. Asking for the Holy Spirit well may be what the author of this book is talking about, that is, the fullness of the Holy Spirit which we can ask for in conversion or after we have been born again and have learned more about the promises of God. And certainly Paul was talking to those who were already true believers when he told them not to be drunk with wine wherein is excess but to be filled with the Spirit. And surely there must be a first time when we are filled and many, many times when we are refilled and filled unto all fullness.

I thoroughly enjoyed this book by an English brother whom I never met and whose earlier writings I have never perused. He has a message we all need to hear and offers to us exciting possibilities of what we can be and do when we open ourselves to the work of the Holy Spirit in our lives. We do not need to agree with him at every point, but in those areas where he speaks and we are doubtful there is always the old adage: Try what he has suggested: you will like it!

Harold Lindsell, Ph.D., D.D., LL.D.

INTRODUCTION

As a young Christian the Spirit had me confused. In one Bible study on Acts chapter two, the group leader said, "Let's not talk about the Holy Spirit. It's too controversial." I didn't know much about the Spirit, but I knew that if he was important in the New Testament, he should be important to me.

Paul seemed to say in Romans 8:9 that I had received the Spirit at conversion. But when I was converted no one said anything about that. Friends made it clear that beliefs need to be based on the sure foundation of Scripture, not on what I happen to feel today. They warned me not to trust emotions, and seemed to put any talk about experiencing the Spirit in that dangerous emotional category.

Emotionalism means putting emotions in charge of beliefs and making them sovereign over Scripture – if I don't *feel* something is true today, then it isn't. Emotionalism means trying to use God like a spiritual valium, a religious "happiness pill" to keep us high and carefree. I knew that such supercharged emotions could be full of sound and fury, but evaporate overnight. They quickly turn as flat as Coca-Cola with the bottle top left undone.

If a VIP had visited our church I would have felt emotion. I certainly expressed emotion seeing my team win the FA Cup. If the Queen had visited the church I cannot imagine how thrilled we all would have been. And like most Englishmen I felt overwhelmed with joy when England won the World Cup. But there was little room in my faith for emotion before the sovereign of the universe, or before Jesus Christ who for us has conquered sin, death and Satan.

I could see the danger of too much emotion more clearly than the danger of too little. My faith and understanding were growing, but were too theoretical, too head-centred. I would probably have doubted the "soundness" of many enthusiastic first-century Christians.

Behind this fear of emotion lay a deeper fear. My concern about charismatics was an excuse. I was afraid of what the Holy Spirit might do to me, and so I tried to keep him at a distance. Hostility to emotion (itself of course emotional), suspicion of experience and fear of the Spirit were drying up the well-springs of my new-found faith.

Many Christians know this ignorance and fear of the Holy Spirit. I wasn't satisfied, and thirsted for something more. Paul explains that this was a preparatory work of the Spirit (Phil 2:13). He encourages us to want to fit into God's ways even when our lives are out of tune with Christ.

I felt stuck, with little sense of direction as a Christian. I could look back to conversion, and know that I was now forgiven and set free by Christ. I knew that Jesus had died for me and that through God's love I had received new birth and eternal life. My life had certainly come to a new beginning, but Sunday services and sermons were growing stale and unreal.

I had lost direction, and though I knew the need for salvation backwards, hearing it over again was becoming less and less important. I didn't know what to do between new birth and paradise.

I began to wish that new birth whisked you straight to heaven, like the express elevator to the top floors of a Manhattan tower block. The weary cry of my heart was, "What next?"

Many have told me since of a similar staleness. Many need to rediscover how Christians are meant to live. Christians in a rut need to be delivered from their weariness to rediscover the adventure of God's glorious and enthralling plans for his children. Above all, that means rediscovering the Holy Spirit.

The first Christians were not bored Christians. They

weren't stuck with that stale and uncomfortable question, "What next?"

I also felt trapped by my own personality. Change just didn't seem possible. No matter how much effort, some old habits and attitudes stubbornly defied every attempt at eviction. Others seemed to disappear for a few weeks or months, only to take up residence again just when I thought I'd got rid of them. Try as I might, I couldn't get clear of the sins that stuck close. My attempts to reflect the positive love of Christ were even more hopeless.

I didn't mention this struggle to anyone else. I didn't mind joining in a general confession of sin. But I was much less keen on being individually identified as a "miserable offender".

What's more, no one else ever mentioned similar difficulties. I thought that must mean the Christian life was as natural for them as it was unnatural for me. Maybe I was a predestined failure! I was tempted to give everything up.

If only I had confessed my difficulties to someone. Perhaps they might have told me a similar story. Not that we are always defeated as Christians, but that change is never complete or easy this side of the grave. We do have to wrestle with the power of sin, but in the power of Christ, not alone in our weakness. We need one eye on the person we used to be, to receive encouragement from any progress, and one eye on Christ, never to lose sight of how far is left to go.

In my defeat, I felt like Jeremiah when he suggested the Israelites were beyond change for the better. He felt their sins were as much part of them as the spots on a leopard; and a leopard cannot change its spots. In our heart of hearts nothing finally changes if we are left to our own strength.

When Jeremiah prophesied the new covenant, he looked forward to the power of God at work in people's hearts, changing them on the inside. No one had told me about that, and no one had told me about the continued struggle of learning to live like Jesus. It was as if the new birth brought forgiveness for the past and a clean sheet, but then it was up to you to change yourself. If only I had seen more clearly!

Jesus' promise

Jesus promised his disciples they would never be left on their own. When he returned to the Father, another Comforter would come. He would be like Jesus and continue his ministry.

The Spirit would not be an optional extra, or the preserve of spiritual specialists. It was only by the Spirit that conversion, discipleship and the new family of Christ could become living realities.

Just as a car is not really a car unless it has an engine, Paul said that without the Spirit, all we have is outward conformity. He called this holding to the form of Christianity but denying its power (2 Tim 3:5).

The first disciples had to wait for the Spirit. They were ordinary men, without outstanding abilities. When they abandoned Jesus at his arrest, their lack of courage left them all shamefaced and Peter in tears. When Mary told them she had seen Jesus risen from the dead, their first reaction was to dismiss it as foolish women's talk. But it was these men Jesus had chosen to turn the world upside down.

Jesus didn't choose the great scholars or the religious high priests. He didn't select men of influence, in good favour with the officials of the Roman Empire. Learning and priestcraft, power and travel were far from the everyday experience of these ordinary men.

Their task was to proclaim the risen Christ and build his Church throughout the world. But first they had to stay in Jerusalem. They had no inner resources which might cause them not to wait. Christ was in charge, and he would send his power from on high, just as he had promised.

Peter's Pentecost sermon took up this theme. It was not

exactly a typical sermon. The fisherman held the crowd spellbound. When he had finished, 3,000 new converts were added to the Church, on its very first day in existence. The power of the Spirit to fulfil the promises of Jesus was beyond any doubt.

Peter explained that lives and worship were being transformed, just as the Old Testament had promised. In that time, the Spirit had fallen on special individuals for a particular task. But Israel's prophets had foretold a new age of the Spirit.

The Spirit would no longer be just with the special few; he would be with all God's people. He would no longer inspire just for a special moment; he would live with and even within God's people for ever. Through signs and wonders, above all the sign of love and the wonder of God's presence, this new beginning would be quite unlike anything ever seen before. The dawn of the new age of the Spirit would be unmistakable.

Peter's message is simple. The new age has begun. God has come down to live with his children.

Peter swiftly changes emphasis to concentrate on Jesus. Jesus had been crucified, but his life was set apart by God. Signs and wonders marked him out as the man of the Spirit, the promised Lord. Raised from the dead and exalted to heaven, he received the Spirit from the Father and now pours out the Spirit on his followers.

Peter's evangelistic invitation brings together his twin themes. His hearers must repent and be baptised in the name of Jesus. They must also receive the promised Holy Spirit.

Only through Jesus' death and resurrection is the Spirit poured out. Only through repentance and faith in Christ is the Spirit received. Life in the Spirit comes through the Lord of the Spirit. The focus of Peter's sermon is not his personal experience, but the cross, because only Jesus' cross makes the new age of the Spirit possible.

What went wrong?

The early Church knew they were the community of the Spirit. If the Spirit had been removed, most of what they were doing would have ground to a halt. If the Holy Spirit was removed from the Church today, would we notice?

As we shall see later, in fact we would. But like Esau we have swapped our birthright for something trivial and passing. He was hungry, and exchanged his privileges as first born son and heir for a bowl of food. We have traded in the glorious inheritance of the Age of the Spirit for a reflection so pale it can almost seem a parody. All we have gained is the passing comfort of social respectability.

Two medieval churchmen watched gold-laden waggons coming into a church treasury. "No longer," one said smugly, "does the Church have to say 'Silver and gold have we none.'" The second replied, "But no more *can* we say, 'In the name of Christ, rise and walk . . .'"

Jesus promised the Holy Spirit would come to unite his disciples. We are the one vine, the one temple, the one family and the one body of Christ. But Christians have often either ignored the Spirit or used him as an excuse to divide from each other.

One of the characteristics of party spirit – a "work of the flesh" (Gal 5:19) – is that any division is completely the fault of the "other side". A friend of mine was asked, "Are you charismatic?" He played safe by asking what they meant. "A church splitter," came the definition . . .

Polite company is meant not to discuss religion and politics. Polite Christian company sometimes feels the same way about the Holy Spirit. The very words "Holy Spirit" can be enough to encourage a stiffening of the spine or even kill conversation. A prickly, forced smile warns you to change the subject fast if you want to preserve the "bond of peace".

Some teaching on the Spirit is detailed on why everyone else is wrong, but doesn't have much positive to say. "Balance" is a crucial word for understanding any biblical teaching, and not just picking the verses you happen to like best. But it can be made to mean "Stay just the way you are."

We all have horror stories about those we disagree with. Jim Packer tells a story of someone who knew two Pentecostal ministers who had left their wives. The man was most frustrated that Packer would not generalise from this vast statistical evidence that this sort of thing was bound to happen if you ever spoke in tongues!

We need desperately to get beyond such factional fighting and prejudice. Our strengths are often close to our weaknesses. Each of us in our worst light could furnish opponents with horror stories. What's more, the best distorted often produces the worst problems. As Shakespeare put it, "Lilies that fester smell far worse than weeds."

Rediscovery

I don't wish for one moment to give the impression of instant or easy answers. In a society of instant food, instant credit, instant everything, we crave an easy way out. That's escapism.

But I do believe my Christian life had been painted into a corner. The frustration and disillusion I felt weren't only the result of pride. They also grew out of incomplete teaching.

Jesus didn't promise the Spirit as an end to all our problems. But he does deliver us from the deadening staleness of a life without purpose. And he does take us beyond the discovery of our lack of inner power. When it seems that our failings will never let us go, we are not left on our own. But to put this into practice, we have to start rediscovering the Spirit.

The Spirit is poured out for every Christian. We need more and more to reclaim the Holy Spirit for the whole Church. Above all, we need more and more to allow the Holy Spirit to reclaim each of us for the Father.

Many Christians recognise that the early Church was

8

alive in the Spirit with a vitality hardly seen today, with a depth of love and power for evangelism. Their example drives us on to something more. The Church has been given the keys to the treasure house of the unsearchable riches of Christ. We cannot afford to busy ourselves with the beauty of the building and never enter inside.

Many Christians are hungry for clear, biblical teaching on the Spirit. Who is he? What is he like? What might he do to me? What about his gifts?

Many want to discover a deeper fulfilment of the New Testament invitation and command to be filled and continue being filled with the Spirit.

Without the Spirit the Word can be dry. Without the Word, things apparently of the Spirit can become bizarre or even dangerous. But we don't have to choose one or the other. The two go together perfectly. As we explore Scripture in the power of the Spirit, together they can bring new maturity.

Evangelistic books are often invaluable for finding out more clearly what the Bible teaches, good reasons for Christian beliefs and what difference it all makes in practice. This book hopes to introduce the Spirit in the same way. Evangelistic books can help Christians know Jesus better. My hope is that you will know the Spirit better through reading this book.

We will bring together biblical teaching and personal testimony to see the impact on everyday living of rediscovering the Spirit. We will examine the teaching honestly, to reach honest and practical conclusions.

God is far more than theory and doctrine, just as love is more than words and talk. That means the Bible is a dangerous book to study. As we seek to rediscover all that the Bible promises about God's Spirit, we can expect him to be changing our lives.

Rob Warner   Easter 1985

Part One

JESUS AND THE SPIRIT

1

THE HOLY "IT"?

I remember wondering as a child who on earth the ghost was which sometimes got a mention in prayers and hymns. I'm sure I wasn't the only one confused.

A ghost is an apparition which may cause fright, but is often no more than a delusion. It is something some people think they experience, which may or may not exist. And so the "Holy Ghost" seems spooky and unreal, a vague presence left behind by Jesus.

Uncertainty about the Spirit has two results. First we become fearful of the Spirit, as if mentioning him might start up a kind of Christian seance. Too much talk about him threatens to turn a church building into a sort of Christian haunted house.

Second, we replace him for all practical purposes in the Trinity with something more familiar. It has been said that many Roman Catholics worship Father, Son and the Holy Virgin; many Anglicans Father, Son and the Holy Church; many Evangelicals Father, Son and the Holy Bible; and many radicals Father, Son and Holy Revolution!

We like to think in pairs. Like love and marriage and the horse and carriage, Father and Son fit together easily in our minds. We even divide the characteristics of the Godhead between these two, with a neatness which goes far beyond the Bible. Judgment pairs with grace, wrath pairs with love, and before we know it we have no room left in our thinking for a third party. The Bible speaks of the love of God and the wrath of God, never of the love of Jesus set against the wrath of the Father, but that's the way many Christians think in practice. Augustine tried to help us out of this corner of two-way thinking by suggesting that the Spirit is the bond of love who unites the other two.

Even the apostles' creed doesn't seem too sure what to say about the Spirit. The sections on the Father and the Son were developed partly to correct various heresies, but the compilers rightly felt much that was positive needed saying. There seems an almost embarrassed silence behind the single, unexplained statement of the third section — "I believe in the Holy Spirit." We do indeed believe, but can nothing more be said than that?

Given this context, it really is no surprise that the most mysterious member of the Trinity is often referred to as "it." "It" is seen as cold and impersonal, or even threatening and a little frightening. "It" can safely and wisely be left to the more emotional, or even the over emotional.

Pentecost is so much more reassuring when referred to as Whit Sunday. After all, the Spirit descended without warning at Pentecost. If that was allowed today, whatever would happen to the order of service?

A friend of ours decided the mysterious "it" was not for her: "Oh, I'm not interested in the Holy Spirit. It isn't my scene at all!"

The alternative to abandoning this mystery is sometimes to recreate him in our own image. If something strange is going on, someone is bound to call it true spirituality.

Some claim to have arrived. A higher plane of Christian living has opened up before them. It is thrilling to hear all that God is doing. But some talk as if the Holy Spirit shut up a small corner shop at the end of the apostolic age, had a brief re-opening at the Reformation, and has now flung open the doors of a fully redeveloped spiritual super-market.

My wife once heard an enthusiastic speaker explain that Spirit-filled Christians don't need holidays. The Spirit simply keeps them going. No biblical evidence was given for this astonishing claim, which came as a relief to me. I rather enjoy holidays, and it had seemed for a moment that my low-level spirituality had been once-for-all exposed!

Neither avoiding the Spirit, nor unbiblical fantasy will do. We need to turn to the Bible. When it comes to the Spirit, most of us think first of Acts or the letters of Paul. We tend to fall into two groups: those who concentrate on the gifts, and those who turn first to the fruit. Our study will begin instead with the teaching of Jesus.

Jesus doesn't talk directly about the gifts, nor does he address the question of one baptism and many fillings. By beginning with Jesus we can set the scene in two chapters and seek to establish much common ground, before turning in chapter three to practical issues. But first of all we need a brief glance at Old Testament teaching about the Spirit. (You may find this section a little heavier than the rest of the book. If so, you may prefer to jump ahead to chapter three, and come back to these pages later.)

The breath of God

The Old Testament doesn't provide a very full picture of the Spirit. What is found there reinforces our sense of mystery. God is beyond us, and other than us. Awe and fear are experienced in his presence. Even his power to forgive causes a response of fear: we all depend on God alone and completely for the forgiveness we need.

Yahweh is present and active in the world. Old Testament writers speak of his finger and his arm, as well as his name and his presence. Their favourite word is *ruach*, which means breath or wind of God.

Genesis chapter one links closely God's breath and God's word. The wind races over the waters as the divine command ("Let there be . . .") brings the created order into being. This is no dull and lifeless explanation of creation, but a hymn of praise to the Lord and Giver of life.

Some suggest this may be an ordinary wind sweeping over the primeval sea of chaos. It seems much more likely that these verses make a deliberate connection between the voice and the breath of the Lord. The voice declares the divine will, even as the breath fulfils those words. God commands and God creates.

By God's breath, life is breathed into man. This doesn't mean that God breathes a little of himself into each living thing. Such pantheism is far from the Old Testament. Rather, God by his Spirit is the source of all life. He is also the sustainer of all life – he keeps everything going. When his breath is withdrawn, life ends. In Ezekiel's vision, the dry bones in the desert seem beyond restoration. It is only by the breath of God that they can be brought back to life (Ezek 37:1–10).

God is still at work in the world. He not only keeps everything going, but he intervenes directly. His involvement in human affairs is both uncontrollable and unpredictable. The earliest Hebrew prophets fell without warning into ecstasy under his breath. When Moses appointed seventy elders, they received a portion of the Spirit and spontaneously began to prophesy. Two of them didn't get to the meeting, but they began to prophesy at exactly the same time (Num 11:24–30).

Samuel once told Saul he would meet a group of prophets and join in their prophesying. Samuel described vividly the irresistible and transforming impact of the Spirit: "The Spirit of the LORD will come upon you in power, and you will . . . be *changed into a different person*" (1 Sam 10:6).

Not even the Temple of Jerusalem can contain God. It was the centre for Israelite worship, but not, in a pagan sense, the place God lives. Solomon's prayer of dedication reaffirms what the book of Deuteronomy had once-for-all declared: no house built by human hands, no matter how ornate and magnificent, not even the ark of God itself, can ever contain the Lord (1 Kings 8:27–30).

Elijah saw God at work in dramatic and sensational ways. Three years' drought followed one of his prayers. Fire from heaven followed another, and discredited the false priests of Baal who were trying to take over Israel. Then a personal death threat arrived from the Queen.

All Elijah's confident public faith evaporated. He fled to the desert, where he prayed for a quick and merciful death.

As a failure, Elijah went deeper into God. He wasn't abandoned in the desert. Instead he was told by an angel to go to the mountain of God, where God would deal with him. At the mountain, in his moment of desperation, he experienced an earthquake, wind and fire; the typical displays of God's judgment and power, and just the kind of thing Elijah had come to expect. But God didn't reveal himself in any of them. The coming of God is not always with a deafening crescendo.

When all grew quiet, Elijah heard a gentle whisper. It was through this still, small voice that God chose to draw near to Elijah. He made it quite clear that Elijah would not be rejected for his failure. Instead, Elijah received instructions for new prophetic tasks. The prophet of thunder discovered a new gentleness, comfort and grace in God, perhaps for the first time (I Kings 17–19).

The Spirit is irresistible. The dominant stress of the Old Testament makes uncomfortable reading for those with tidy minds who want God kept under firm control. Old Testament experience of the Spirit shows that God is not always orderly and a respecter of human conventions. Yet the story of Elijah is a crucial corrective for those with tornado temperaments. God does not only speak in a loud voice. Nor is the reality of our worship measured in decibels. The wind blows where it will, not where our rubric or tradition prefers.

The Old Testament never suggests God's presence is experience for experience sake. There is always a moral force to moments of inspiration. God's invasion of holy power comes upon a few for the benefit of many.

Military leaders are inspired for holy war which ensures the purity of Israel. Kings are anointed for right ruling as God's special representatives. Prophets are inspired to demand moral goodness in private, commercial, and political dealings. When Yahweh breathes, leaders and spokesmen for true holiness step from anonymity into the public eye. Their new authority is unmistakable.

God's breath is seen in human experience and action, but above all in the sacred writings. The breath of God is given voice as he speaks through the classical prophets. These books are not monochrome in what they say or how they say it. Inspiration is not presented in terms of God dictating to a prophetic secretary, but in terms of double authorship. The words have the authority of Yahweh, and yet they are stamped with the style and emphasis of the individual prophet.

The Spirit seems rather remote in his unpredictable power. His presence as wind and fire underlines this otherness. A third description reveals a new stress. Streams will flow in the desert. The water of life will be poured out. Israel will be a watered garden before her God (Isa 58:11).

The prophets anticipate a breakthrough to a new age of renewal and holiness. A future king, uniquely filled with the Spirit, will bring this about. At that time, but not before, the Spirit will inspire all believers, and not just a few. Jeremiah even hints at an end to the ancient Israelite priesthood (Jer 31:34).

In this new age, God's moral power will make inner change possible. Jeremiah reports that God will write his law on human hearts (Jer 31:33). Ezekiel promises a heart of flesh will replace our hearts of stone (Ezek 36:36). In both expressions the same meaning is clear: God will be changing people on the inside in a remarkable new way.

The Spirit who is the source of life will make possible the renewal of life. There will be no preferential treatment for kings, priests or prophets. The Spirit will fall on *all* believers.

Isaiah was almost overwhelmed by his vision of the glory of the Lord shining throughout the Temple at Jerusalem. He was caught up into the heavenly adoration of God's majesty and holiness. At the same time, the vision brought home as never before Isaiah's own sinfulness, and his desperate need of forgiveness. The presence of God is glorious, but by no means always comfortable (Isa 6:1–8).

When Isaiah saw the holiness of God, he experienced judgment. In the age to come, mankind would at last experience lasting deliverance from sin, and inner moral transformation. Only in the fulfilment of this promise could the human heart truly be changed. Only then could Jeremiah's leopard change its spots.

The personal Spirit

The fragmentary insights of the Old Testament reveal the mystery, unpredictability, moral power and promise which attach to the elusive breath of God. For a full account of the Spirit, we have to turn to the New Testament. In the Gospels, the teaching of the Old Testament is maintained and yet brought to new heights of clarity and detail.

Jesus begins his public ministry by reading from Isaiah. In him the prophecy is fulfilled. The good news is preached to the poor, and the captives are set free. The anointed King of the new age has come.

With Nicodemus, Jesus discussed the need for spiritual rebirth. Man's destiny is not based on religious pedigree or social respectability. Only those born of the Spirit can enter the Kingdom of Heaven. He also takes up the theme of the Spirit's unpredictability. All those born of the Spirit can expect to live out surprises from God (John 3:8).

In Jesus' last week in Jerusalem he spoke about the Spirit more than ever before. This is found in great detail in John 12–16. Caiaphas had said with unconscious foresight that the death of Jesus would be expedient to avoid further bloodshed (John 11:50). Now Jesus reveals the true expediency of his coming crucifixion. His death would make possible the dawn of a new era. His departure is necessary so that the Spirit may come (John 16:7).

Although the disciples grieved already at the coming loss, they would not be left on their own. Far from making do with only memories of the good old days, they would accomplish even greater things than Jesus (John 14:12). This hardly meant they would achieve more because they were many and Jesus was one. Jesus promised that they would receive his Spirit and perform mighty acts in his name.

Throughout John's Gospel, Jesus refers to God as "the Father" and as "the one who sent me". In the teaching of this last week parallel phrases are now used about the Spirit:

I will ask the Father, and he will give you another Counsellor (John 14:16)

. . . the Holy Spirit, whom the Father will send in my name . . . (John 14:26)

When the Counsellor comes, whom I will send to you from the Father, the Spirit of truth who goes out from the Father . . . (John 15:26)

Unless I go away, the Counsellor will not come to you; but if I go, I will send him to you (John 16:7).

John confirms time and again that Jesus is Lord of the Spirit, and that the Spirit's coming is only possible through the death of Jesus. What's more, the Spirit is sent at the request of Jesus, and comes like Jesus, from the Father.

This is the most developed thinking about the Trinity in the New Testament. Jesus and the Father are one. All that belongs to Jesus belongs to the Father. And the Spirit will not act independently, but will make known all that belongs to Jesus, just as Jesus has only acted according to the will of the Father. The activity of the three is distinct and yet indivisibly one.

We need to pause on John's deliberate and emphatic underlining of Jesus' message. The Old Testament leaves open the possibility of referring to the Spirit as "it". John reveals that Jesus denied this categorically for all who follow him.

John could have referred to the Spirit as "it". In fact, according to Greek grammar he should have. Just as table in French is feminine – "la table" or "elle" – in Greek spirit is neuter, "to pneuma" or "auto". When John mentions "the Spirit", he uses the correct neuter form of "the". But where grammar requires him to say "it", John deliberately wrote "*he*".

You can imagine the shock for his first readers. It would have been as unmistakable as when an Englishman shouts (the English always assume that foreigners are a little deaf) "le table" or "il". The nearest in English would be to write in capital letters: HE.

This is no accident on John's part. He deliberately adjusts grammar to draw attention to good theology. He wants to be faithful above all to the teaching of Jesus. And so John stresses as strongly as he can, *the Holy Spirit is not "it", but "HE"*.

The Spirit is not a sanctifying spectre about which we cannot be too sure. He retains all his Old Testament qualities, but the Holy Spirit is a person. He is as personal as Jesus, and he is as much God as the Son and the Father are God. Anything less than this emphasis is less than Jesus intended. Anything less fails to capture the first principle of Jesus' teaching on the promised Spirit. "Unless I go away, the Counsellor will not come to you; but if I go, I will send him to you" (John 16:7).

What is the Spirit like?

The Spirit may be personal, and even God, but what is God like? Faced with the infinite God, the most profound human thinkers are soon out of their depth. To the psalmist, such knowledge is beyond his reach – "it is too lofty" (Ps 139:6).

Isaiah stressed this great chasm between man and God. Our thoughts are not his thoughts, nor our ways his ways (Isa 55:8). Men before God are no greater than grasshoppers – our behaviour is as insignificant as an insect's scurrying (Isa 40:22). Even the great nations are like dust on the scales (Isa 40:15).

This leaves us with an enormous problem. God reveals himself through his actions, through the Bible and through his people. We are bound to want to talk about him. The need to describe him is part of the need to know him. But where do we begin?

One solution is to play the big word game. The more syllables in a word, the more profound it can seem. Soon a collection appears – omnipresent, omniscient, omnipotent. Someone even wrote a hymn about the co-eternal consubstantial Trinity. These words have their place, but they soon leave most of us with verbal indigestion. God is personal. That's why Jesus taught in parables and not in complex abstractions. That doesn't mean abstractions are useless, but they are not very good at communicating a living relationship.

Philip the apostle shared our problem. Jesus had spoken a great deal about the Father, but Philip still found it too abstract, and so he said, "Lord, show us the Father, and that will be enough for us" (John 14:8).

Jesus' reply is a breakthrough. He didn't reflect on the otherness of God or his transcendence of human categories. Nor did God manifest himself in the room or on the clouds. Rather, Jesus revealed himself to be the supreme revelation of the character and will of God.

Jesus spoke so bluntly it would have been blasphemy on anyone else's lips. He didn't say I am the kind of person that shows God best. The identification was absolute: "Anyone who has seen me has seen the Father" (John 14:9).

This is the very heart of the gospel. If you want to know what God is like, look to Jesus. If you want to know God's response to our sin, look to Jesus. If you want to see God reconciling the world to himself, look to Jesus. For in Jesus, "all the fullness of the Deity lives in bodily form" (Col 2:9).

There is only a small step from this to our present theme. The Spirit is personal and has the same origin as Jesus. The Spirit reveals Jesus and is sent by him. And so, if we want to know what the Spirit is like, we need above all to consider Jesus, as he is portrayed in the four Gospels.

This close identification of the Spirit with Jesus provides much reassurance. It takes us right away from super-supernaturalism that wants to leave Jesus behind and pass to higher things. The New Testament declares with one voice: there is no higher revelation than Jesus Christ, and Jesus promised the Spirit.

God's best gift

Luke's Gospel is the gospel of the Spirit and of joy. Luke records that Jesus assured his disciples that the gift of the Spirit can be welcomed with open arms because God is the supremely loving Father.

The humour and caricature of this story are typical of Jesus. We can be sure that as many children endlessly demanded things from their fathers then as do now. Perhaps it's because Dad is seen as a soft touch, but holiday resorts and supermarkets echo with the same request: "Daddy, *please* may I have just one more!"

Jesus shows how perverse it would be to betray a child's simple trust. In his story, each request of the child is met with the wrong gift. What's more, each gift offered is at best useless, and at worst positively dangerous. A request for bread earns a stone, a fish wins a serpent and an egg gains a scorpion. The humour is clear. No decent human father would consistently betray good requests with dangerous gifts (Luke 11:11–12).

Then Jesus adds a double twist. Human fathers don't always live up to what they know is right, but at least they know in theory how to give good gifts. In fact, men have this knowledge, and even give good things to their children, despite being "evil" (Luke 11:13). God's goodness exceeds man's by more than the gift of bread exceeds a stone. Jesus gives a ringing affirmation to the incomparable goodness of the heavenly Father.

While Matthew takes the story that far, Luke remembers

the decisive punchline. Both are agreed that Jesus encouraged prayer for good things and promised such prayer
would be answered. Both are agreed that God's gifts are
gifts of grace, given through his love, and not because we
deserve rewards. But Luke recognises that Jesus taught
that the gift of the Holy Spirit was the best good gift of all.
The Spirit is the supreme expression of God's fatherliness
to those who follow Jesus.

Once again, Jesus' teaching centres on the promise of the
Spirit. He provides all the reassurance we could possibly
need about the goodness of God's precious gift: "how much
more will your Father in heaven give the Holy Spirit to
those who ask him" (Luke 11:13).

Another counsellor

Some friends of ours were legal guardians to another
couple's children. That couple were tragically killed while
abroad. Our friends could never replace the children's real
parents. But they stood in their place. Nothing could make
up for the terrible loss, but the children knew they would
never be abandoned. Their foster parents would do everything for them that they possibly could.

The disciples were faced with a similarly devastating loss.
For three years they had been led and taught by Jesus. They
had given up their jobs to travel where he travelled. Now
they had arrived in Jerusalem, and the sense of adventure
was upon them. Following the triumphal entry of King
Jesus, things were bound to come to a head.

They listened to Jesus with bated breath and all their
hopes were dashed. The Romans would stay in Israel.
Jewish religion would not be reformed. The Master had
come to the City of God not to reign on earth, but to die.
When the disciples were thoroughly dismayed, Jesus gave
his fullest explanation of what the Holy Spirit is like.

Jesus promised the disciples they would never be left on
their own. His departure will mean the coming of another
counsellor (John 14:16). Jesus could have meant a different

counsellor of a different kind. The word John uses in Greek has a distinct stress – the new counsellor will be another *of the same kind*.

What follows reinforces this meaning. The new counsellor will be another like Jesus. In fact, so faithfully will the Spirit reveal Jesus and glorify him, he may be described as "the presence of Jesus when Jesus is absent" (R. E. Brown).

John's Greek word for counsellor is very rich in meaning. The AV translation – comforter – carried the long-lost emphasis of bringing the strength needed for action. The Spirit of Jesus is not simply "gentle, meek and mild", any more than the New Testament calls the followers of Jesus to be "little sunbeams"!

Jim Packer cast a wide net round the meaning of "paraclete" with the following list: comforter, strengthener, counsellor, helper, supporter, adviser, advocate, ally, senior friend (*Keep in Step with the Spirit*, Leicester 1984). The Spirit comes alongside the disciples of Jesus to continue Jesus' own ministry. His particular help will reflect our particular need.

Lesslie Newbigin provided a complementary net of meanings: the Spirit calls, beseeches, entreats, comforts, consoles, exhorts. He adds that these words sum up the "very stuff of the Christian life together" – "no human achievement but as a gift from the Father" (*The Light Has Come*, Grand Rapids 1982).

The only other use of "paraclete" is in 1 John 2:1. There the paraclete is Jesus, who speaks in our defence before the Father. This confirms the protective role of the Spirit. He is the best defender of the faith, both within our hearts and before the world. He is another comforter even as Jesus is the first comforter.

The promise of Jesus goes far beyond providing a substitute for himself, or an equivalent to a legal guardian. As Christ has been for three years to his disciples, even so will the Spirit be in the future. He will be the presence of Jesus for them and for all Christians, not just for three years, but to the end of the age.

Each year after the crucifixion would seem to take the apostles further from Jesus. The death of each apostle would seem to take the early Christians still further away from him. And each generation that followed would have a still less certain grasp on the Saviour.

Not so, Jesus explained! Because the Spirit is "another Jesus", as the Spirit illumines Scripture and inspires our hearts, Jesus is ever present with us. The quite astonishing promise is that the presence of Jesus will never fade away. That doesn't mean we don't need the Gospels: they have been given as the authoritative record of Jesus' life and teaching for every generation. But in every generation, informed by those gospels, the presence of Jesus will remain just as real.

If we want to know what God is like, we look to Jesus. If we want to understand the ministry of the Spirit, we look to Jesus. Nowhere is Jesus seen more clearly as the counsellor than in the last week before his crucifixion. The quiet, reassuring confidence of his words brought peace to his disciples then, and has spoken afresh to every generation of disciples since: "Do not let your hearts be troubled. Trust in God; trust also in me" (John 14:1).

The mystery of the Spirit can make us fearful. We either run fast from him, or we remake him in the image of our own experiences. Jesus shows us a better way by explaining his person and ministry for us. In the Spirit Jesus meets us. He neither gift wraps our faults nor manhandles our frailties. But by pointing us to the love of the Father, just as Jesus did for the disciples, he meets our deepest needs.

Experiencing the Spirit doesn't mean experiencing some vague impersonal force. The Spirit who continues the ministry of Jesus is like Jesus. The glorious confidence of the New Testament is this: to experience the Spirit is nothing less than to experience Jesus.

We began with the mystery of the Spirit. Now is a good moment to sum up our key discoveries so far:

* The Spirit is the power of God. He is at work in the world. He doesn't offer experience for experience sake, but his presence brings moral direction.

* The Spirit is personal. He is like Jesus. He is sent from the Father who can be trusted to give good things.

* The Spirit continues the ministry of Jesus. He is given through the death and resurrection of Jesus. To experience the Spirit is to experience Jesus the Lord.

2

THE SPIRIT OF JESUS

I will always remember children's cinema on Saturday mornings. You could hardly hear the soundtrack for the noise. We screamed and we cheered, we groaned and we booed. The building seemed to echo with the munching of innumerable crisps.

Someone was always being gently escorted out by the scruff of the neck for kissing the girls or puffing a furtive cigarette in the dark. The excitement always mounted, whatever the distractions. The programme was getting nearer and nearer its climax – Dick Barton, Special Agent.

No matter how cruel the bad guys, no matter how fiendish their plots, Dick would win through. No matter how deadly their traps, just when it seemed impossible to survive, he escaped . . . but not until the next episode. Two generations or more of British boys grew up with the same dream: they would be like Dick Barton when they grew up, or at least become like Snowy, his faithful assistant.

Not all our heroes last. Dick must now be confined to libraries of old black and white films. Most children apparently lose two other idols between the ages of about five and eight. Mummy and Daddy aren't perfect after all. They not only make mistakes, they can't even always tell when you blame it all on your little brother.

Like it or not, we still have heroes in later years. I don't just mean people we admire, but people we would love to be like. Americans rather grandly call them "role models".

There is probably a generation of British wives and mothers for whom Margaret Thatcher is now a role model. Living rooms resound with a new phrase during domestic disputes over what wallpaper to choose or where to go on holiday: "There is no alternative!"

As Christians too we have our heroes. There are leaders and preachers we pay particular attention to, and churches we would like to be part of or wish our own churches to learn from.

It may be someone like David Watson, who went to an almost empty church with the official task of closing it down. Instead he saw it transformed by the grace of God into a beacon of spiritual renewal, to which visitors came from all over the world. It may be someone like Jackie Pullinger or David Wilkerson, who proclaim the power of Christ to no-hopers, drug addicts and prostitutes, and see wretched lives healed. Or it may be someone like Corrie ten Boom, who learnt to forgive the Nazis who imprisoned her at Ravensbruck concentration camp, or Maximilian Kolbe, who substituted himself for a Jew under Nazi death sentence, and was executed in his place.

We are surrounded by an ever-growing great cloud of witnesses (Heb 12:1). It is good to have examples to follow, since they help us to see how to live as Christians in today's world. But we must watch out for hero-worship. Even the best of our heroes have feet of clay. Idols set up on pedestals are sure to bring disappointment in the end.

When it comes to the Holy Spirit, each of us needs to ask, "Who are my role models?" Once again it is natural to have modern examples to follow. The curious thing is that we don't go straight to the obvious answer. We buff up the shine on our particular heroes, yet the answer of the New Testament is plain. Jesus is our "role model" for being filled with the Spirit.

At first sight this may need justifying. The Spirit is only mentioned a handful of times in Matthew and Mark. But a theme's importance is not necessarily measured by how often it appears. In a symphony, a brief phrase in the first movement may prepare the way for a key theme later. It takes only a few seconds to score a goal, but that's the most important moment in a football match. We need to recognise two key reasons for the way the gospels present the Spirit:

1 The task of the Spirit is to glorify Christ
The disciples followed this pattern by concentrating on the single, glorious focus of Christ. Nothing could be allowed to distract, no matter how important, from Jesus as Lord.

The gift of the Spirit came through the Son. His presence is therefore derivative, rather than an alternative to Christ-centred Christianity. The Spirit is by no means supplementary to the work of the Son, as if grace in Christ was somehow incomplete and needed topping up.

In Christ are found *all* the unsearchable riches of heaven. In Christ *alone* is deliverance from sin and adoption into God's new family. In Christ *alone* is complete salvation, and the coming of the Spirit is part of this glorious gift of grace.

2 The Spirit didn't just glorify the exalted Christ. He revealed and explained Jesus of Nazareth
The Spirit made possible the first Christians' life together. By the Spirit they knew the presence of God, and discovered they could exercise the power of God. The Spirit was the known quantity of present experience, but, as Jesus had promised, he constantly prompted the Christians to proclaim Jesus Christ.

The task of the gospels was to preserve and explore this central focus. Jesus' life and teaching didn't just matter, they were *crucial*. So was his double identity as perfect man and only Son of God. Only in the light of Jesus could the reality and validity of present experience be explained. Only through proclaiming Jesus could their present experience of the Spirit be entered into by others.

The gospel-writers didn't want first to stress Jesus as the master of spirituality, in prayer and holy living. He was these things, but above all he was the God-man, in whom God was reconciling the world to himself.

The man of the Spirit

The fires of prophecy had not been rekindled for generations. Israel under Roman occupation still suffered a famine of the Word of the Lord. God had entered a self-imposed silence. Yet hope in the Messiah remained keen. The presence of the Romans as yet another army of occupation intensified the ancient yearning for deliverance, and for the promised age to come. "How long, O Lord?" was the question on the lips of many faithful Jews.

With the baptism of Jesus, the new age is revealed. God's new beginning is declared to all. John the Baptist had called the people back to God and to his holiness. He described himself as the forerunner, preparing the way for the Lord. As Jesus stands in the Jordan, the waters of baptism running through his beard, the promise of the prophets is fulfilled. The Spirit of the Lord has come upon his chosen one and the age of the kingdom has dawned. As Jesus put it: "The time is fulfilled and the kingdom of God is at hand; repent, and believe the gospel" (Mark 1:15 RSV).

The anointing of the Spirit begins Jesus' public ministry. His secret years of quiet preparation are over. In God's time he is sent out with the message that will finally take him to Golgotha, the place of execution.

Before this public life wins followers and provokes enemies, the Spirit drives Jesus out into the wilderness. Intense solitary prayer and spiritual warfare are necessary marks of the new age.

The voice from heaven declared the unique role of the God-man. Almost immediately the voice of the tempter tries out the true humanity of Jesus. He was "tempted in every way, just as we are" (Heb 4:15). Whatever the assault, Jesus' purity remained undefiled: he "was without sin" (Heb 4:15).

The wilderness experience prepared and strengthened Jesus for the three years ahead. Matthew and Mark both stress the authority of Jesus' conflict with demons. Jesus possessed the power of the Spirit as no man ever had before.

Matthew adds some distinctive extras to the message of Mark. He is always concerned to stress Jesus' fulfilment of Old Testament prophecy. In the great moments of his life and in the tiniest detail, Jesus is always and unmistakably revealed as the Messiah.

Between the temptations and the beginning of Jesus' preaching, Matthew inserts a prophecy from Isaiah: "the people living in darkness have seen a great light; on those living in the land of the shadow of death a light has dawned" (Isa 9:2; Matt 4:16). In Jesus the promised hope has dawned. Anointed with the Spirit, Jesus radiates the holy presence of God upon the "people living in darkness". The Messiah has come.

Matthew stresses two more key insights, one at each end of his gospel. First, he provides some extra detail about Jesus' conception. Some people wanted to see Jesus as just another good man. For them, it was only when the Spirit descended at his baptism that Jesus became any different to the rest of us. At that point, because he had been so good, God decided to appoint him Messiah, and even adopt him as Son. Matthew will have none of that.

The breath of God creates Jesus in the womb, but not as just another life. Jesus has no earthly father. Mary is "with child through the Holy Spirit" (Matt 1:18). This is stressed again in a similar phrase two verses later, by recording the words from Joseph's reassuring dream: "the angel of the Lord . . . said . . . what is conceived in her is from the Holy Spirit" (Matt 1:20).

John and Paul both go into greater detail by revealing the pre-existence of the Son of God. The Son has always been God, and there was never a time when he did not exist. He didn't suddenly arise at the moment of conception. Rather, at this moment, the divine Son took upon himself his human nature.

Matthew's stress is emphatic. The Spirit didn't come upon Jesus for the first time at his baptism. From the beginning of the incarnation, Jesus had continually been the unique man of the Spirit.

In the closing verses of his gospel, Matthew records the great commission: "Therefore go and make disciples of all nations, baptising them in the name of the Father and of the Son and of the Holy Spirit, and teaching them to obey everything I have commanded you" (Matt 28:19–20).

John's baptism had been a baptism of repentance, turning away from the old life. Christian baptism would be a baptism into the new life. The Spirit is set alongside the Father and the Son in a remarkable departure from Jewish practice. All three are to be worshipped as the one God, and all three are involved in salvation. For Jesus, and for Matthew, the Church is inseparable from the Spirit, and the Spirit is inseparable from the task of mission.

A promise follows the great commission, and with it Matthew ends his gospel. Jesus assures his disciples of his permanent presence with them: "And surely I will be with you always, to the very end of the age" (Matt 28:20).

The promise needs no explanation from Matthew. His first readers could move directly from the words of Jesus to their present experience. Jesus is with them all, not just as an idea to write theology about, nor just as an example to follow. He is present in person. The man of the Spirit, through the gift of his Spirit, is experienced here and now as their living Lord.

Luke fills in much more detail, as he confirms that Jesus brings about the new age of the Spirit. In his opening chapter, the birth of Jesus is heralded by the re-awakening of the gift of prophecy. The silence of the Spirit in Israel is broken. As Elizabeth and Zechariah prophesy they are full of the Holy Spirit (Luke 1:41, 67). But their inspiration is only for that special moment. Their experience follows the Old Testament pattern.

The coming of the Spirit on Mary is linked directly to the holy name of the Son (Luke 1:35). John the Baptist grows in the Spirit as a child (Luke 1:80). But while Jesus grows physically like any other child, he already has absolute fullness of the Spirit (Luke 2:40).

Immediately following the baptism, Luke confirms the

permanent special quality of Jesus' life. Jesus is "full of the Holy Spirit" and is "led by the Spirit in the desert" (Luke 4:1). When he returns from the temptations, he comes "in the power of the Spirit" (Luke 4:14). When he reads in the synagogue at Nazareth, he not only claims to be a prophet (Luke 4:24), but The Prophet, upon whom the Spirit of the Lord has come, and in whom the ancient words of Isaiah are fulfilled (Luke 4:21). This repetition, right at the beginning of Jesus' ministry, is deliberate and unmistakable: at all times Jesus is empowered and filled with the Spirit.

The declaration at Nazareth was outrageous to Jesus' neighbours. How dare anyone make such a claim! This was the first time the authorities tried to kill Jesus. The fullness of the Spirit was already proving dangerous.

Luke makes it perfectly clear that Jesus is the unique man of the Spirit. Through him the wholeness, freedom and true deliverance of the Messianic age become possible. Only with Jesus is the presence and fullness of the Spirit permanent. Peter later summed it up preaching to Cornelius: "how God anointed Jesus with the Holy Spirit and power" (Acts 10:38).

The man of the Spirit reveals the permanent presence of the Spirit that the prophets had promised. The Spirit equips for public ministry, protects in temptation, empowers for teaching and healing, and guides in all things. In the Spirit, Jesus lived a life of love and prayer, with a remarkable freedom from normal human fears and anxieties. In his confident sense of the presence of God, the chasm between God and ordinary human experience is bridged.

God can be with us all the time in our everyday lives. Only through Jesus and only by the Spirit is this made possible.

Jesus didn't offer super-supernaturalism – a life full of visions and no holidays. Nor did he offer respectable conformity – just like everyone else with extra religious trimmings. But he did show us what kind of life can be lived in the power of the Spirit.

The gospels are unanimous. Life in the new age of the Spirit means living like Jesus. If you want to know what a Spirit-filled, Spirit-led life is like, look to Jesus. When you want a role model for spiritual living, don't look first to your modern heroes. Turn instead to Jesus, the man of the Spirit.

The Lord of the Spirit

Family stories make two kinds of successful television. As the family saga unfolds, the generations pass by. Family likenesses continue, as the tragedy of one generation becomes the triumph of the next. Across the world many millions were glued to their TV sets for *The Jewel in the Crown* and for *Roots*. One of the earlier TV triumphs, *The Forsyte Saga*, rumbled on for countless weeks charting one family through the Victorian era. It reached parts of the world untouched even by the British Empire it brought back to life.

The other kind of family success is of course the soap opera. Here the characters seem never to grow old. If an actor gets sick he risks being killed off, but the deaths are almost always off screen. *Dallas* and *Dynasty* have run for year after year. Their secret of almost eternal success seems to be vast allowances for high fashion clothing, plenty of make-up and voluminous wigs. *Dr. Who* was given a different secret of almost eternal life. The actor's face changed five times in about twenty years, but the plot stayed just the same.

Some Christians think Luke's two books are like a family saga. The first volume tells us what Jesus said and did. The second takes us beyond Jesus to tell the story of the Spirit. Such a rigid distinction is a big mistake.

For Luke, as for the other New Testament writers, the story remains the same. The Church belongs to Jesus. The Church's experience of the power of the Spirit is only possible through what Jesus has done, and what's more, it is Jesus who now pours out the Spirit on his Church. With his resurrection and ascension, the Man of the Spirit has also become the Lord of the Spirit.

All four gospels establish this truth even before Jesus' public ministry begins. John the Baptist says he will be followed by the one who will "baptise with the Spirit". In fulfilment of the ancient prophecies, Jesus will have the authority to pour out the power of God. But during his earthly life, Jesus makes no attempt to do this.

This close link between the Spirit and the risen Lord is found throughout the New Testament. For Paul, the Spirit can be referred to as the "Spirit of the Lord" (2 Cor 3:17), "the Spirit of his Son" (Gal 4:16), and even the "Spirit of Jesus Christ" (Phil 1:19). Peter also refers to the "Spirit of Christ" (1 Pet 1:11). The Spirit has been poured into our hearts (Rom 5:5), and yet Paul can also refer to "Christ in you, the hope of glory" (Col 1:27). The two are inseparable for Paul and also for John, who writes of the Spirit in our hearts (1 John 4:13) and also Christ within us (1 John 5:12).

At the same time, Christ and the Spirit remain distinct. The Spirit is how Christ is with us. He by no means distracts us from the historical death and resurrection, nor from Jesus' present authority as Lord of all.

This closeness of the Spirit and Jesus, and Jesus' role as Lord of the Spirit, are spelt out at the end of Luke's Gospel and the beginning of Acts. Jesus had taught that the Spirit would provide the disciples with the right words before rulers and authorities (Luke 12:11–12). In his last week in Jerusalem, Jesus adds that he will provide such words of wisdom himself (Luke 21:14–25). The role is the same, and Jesus will fulfil his own task by means of the Spirit.

After his resurrection, Jesus promises the disciples will be "clothed with power from on high" (Luke 24:49). Then, just before the ascension, he recalls the prophecy of John the Baptist, and declares that their baptism with the Spirit is at hand (Acts 1:5). Finally, he explains how these twin hopes fit together: "you will receive power when the Holy Spirit comes on you" (Acts 1:8).

As in John's gospel, it is Jesus who will send the Spirit.

The Spirit is Jesus' parting gift to his disciples, the way the Church is brought to life, and the means of continuing Jesus' own ministry. Not until they receive the Spirit's power will the disciples become effective witnesses to Jesus.

We looked earlier at Peter's Pentecost sermon. He began with the disciples' spectacular new experience, but soon switched to Christ as his central theme. Again this ties in with Jesus' own words. Witness must wait for the Spirit. What they witness to first is not their personal experience of the Spirit, or their new sense of joy or fulfilment: the gospel they proclaim centres on Christ crucified and raised.

Christian witness should always be Christ centred. Its focus is the historical means of salvation, brought about by God for those who could not save themselves. Jesus summed this up in his resurrection appearance on the Emmaus Road: "The Christ will suffer and rise from the dead on the third day, and repentance and forgiveness of sins will be preached in his name to all nations, beginning at Jerusalem. You are witnesses of these things" (Luke 24:46–9).

At the climax of his sermon, Peter gets to the heart of this great truth. Jesus is not merely a good example. He was the unique Man of the Spirit, "accredited by God to you by miracles, wonders and signs" (Acts 2:36). More than that, he is now the Lord of the Spirit. Only through Jesus, crucified and risen, is there forgiveness and new life. Only through Jesus can the Spirit be received. For only Jesus, exalted as Lord, pours out the Spirit on his Church: "Exalted to the right hand of God, he has received from the Father the promised Holy Spirit and has poured out what you now see and hear" (Acts 2:33).

Many have said that Luke's second book would be best entitled the Acts of the Holy Spirit. Without the Spirit there could have been no Church. Without the Spirit the apostles could not have begun their magnificent achievements. Luke undoubtedly champions the vital presence and power of the Spirit.

It may come as a surprise to discover that Luke suggests a

36

different title for Acts. In the very first verse he refers back to his Gospel. Volume one, he reminds the reader, covered the period up to Jesus' ascension. Then he uses an unexpected phrase. His gospel was not simply an account of what Jesus did and taught. It actually reported what Jesus "*began* to do and to teach" (Acts 1:1).

Luke's confidence in both the personal experience of the Spirit and the objective Lordship of Christ leads him to a remarkable claim. His ringing conviction is that Jesus is alive. More than that, through the power of the Spirit, Luke's second book records not merely the story of his followers but the *continued* actions and teachings of the Lord Christ. It is the Acts of Jesus Christ, volume two.

Some Christians talk as if they would prefer to do without the Spirit. They want Jesus, but no more than him. Others talk as if they want to graduate from Jesus to the Spirit. Neither group has a biblical leg to stand on. Jesus is Lord of the Spirit.

There is no either/or attitude in the New Testament: either Jesus or the Spirit. For the early Christians that would be impossible nonsense. Jesus and the Spirit go together. Quite simply, you can't have one without the other.

The Spirit and Jesus

My wife and I used to live in York. The land there is fairly flat, and the city planners to their great credit have restricted the height of new buildings to preserve the medieval skyline as much as possible. Over the city towers York Minster, one of the most beautiful Gothic cathedrals in the world.

At night the Minster is floodlit. You can see it clearly from well beyond York's ancient city walls. The building is so vast that from a distance it seems almost to hover above the city. The warm yellow stonework has an unforgettable glow.

In my mind's eye I can always see that majestic vision.

The ideal of the medieval craftsmen has been preserved and enhanced. As if set on a hill, even at night the Minster's breath-taking grandeur eloquently declares the glory of God.

Modern floodlights are nothing like the sweeping searchlights used in film titles by Twentieth Century Fox. They are discreetly concealed and precisely directed. They neither draw attention to themselves nor bathe in light the night sky or buildings beyond their "target". Those in York superbly glorify the Minster, but never draw attention to themselves.

This is how the Spirit relates to Jesus. He has a divine floodlight ministry. He lights up the glory of the Son. Writing to the Corinthians, Paul revealed that the Christian message met with great resistance (1 Cor 1:18–25). To the Jews, a crucified Saviour was a stumbling block. The law said a man hung on a tree was cursed (Deut 21:23). Surely Jesus could not be the Messiah? To the Greeks, the idea of God revealing salvation in an insignificant rural backwater of the Roman Empire was foolishness. Could one die for many? Surely classical philosophy was the summit of human wisdom!

Reactions to the gospel don't change much. Today some dismiss as foolish the idea that God loves us so much he intervened in human history. Others, with misplaced confidence that man can save himself, turn away proudly from Christ's offer of salvation. Now as much as then, Paul's words remain true: "the foolishness of God is wiser than man's wisdom, and the weakness of God is stronger than man's strength" (1 Cor 1:25). Paul is at pains to stress that he doesn't attempt to evangelise by using tricks of speech, emotional pressure or any display of learning. There is only one way to communicate Christ, and that goes way beyond any human skill. Paul's evangelism comes with "a demonstration of the Spirit's power" (1 Cor 2:4). It was through Paul that the Corinthians were pointed to Christ and found faith, but the power came from God (1 Cor 2:5).

Only the Spirit can floodlight the message of the cross,

turning it from "foolishness" into "to us who are being saved the power of God" (1 Cor 1:18). Only God has "made foolish the wisdom of the world" (1 Cor 1:20). He has done it through his unmerited love in sending his Son to die for us.

Just as conversion is brought about by God, not man, confession of faith is only possible through the Spirit. Paul sums up his message in a simple but life-changing phrase: ". . . if you confess with your mouth 'Jesus is Lord', and believe in your heart that God raised him from the dead, you will be saved" (Rom 10:9).

Paul's test for preaching and prophecy centres on the same confession. Only by the Spirit could Jesus be confessed as Lord (1 Cor 12:3). John also provides a test of true Christianity. He concentrates on the incarnation, because some super-spiritualisers were saying that Jesus was a spirit, and not a real human: "This is how you can recognise the Spirit of God: Every Spirit that acknowledges that Jesus Christ has come in the flesh is from God, but every spirit that does not acknowledge Jesus is not from God. This is the spirit of the antichrist . . ." (1 John 4:2–3). Only by the floodlight ministry of the Spirit can people be pointed to Jesus as Lord, both in conversion and in continued confession of faith.

For the fullest exploration of this floodlight ministry, we need to return to John's gospel. When Jesus promises the Spirit, he directly links the Spirit's coming with the realisation "on that day" that "I am in my Father and you are in me" (John 14:20). Jesus' divinity and every Christian's new status in him are both revealed by the Spirit.

A few verses later, the Spirit's crucial role in the composition of the gospels is revealed. The Spirit will not dictate the gospels, somehow taking over the evangelists, but he will light up in the memories of the eyewitnesses all that Jesus taught. The result won't be a dead tradition, locked into mere information about the past. The Spirit will also illumine those memories, explaining their significance and applying them to the Church (John 14:26).

The Spirit is the reason for the authority and up-to-dateness of the Bible. He has inspired writings that are uniquely and universally true. He also has the power to make them directly and personally relevant. In every generation, from all sorts of backgrounds, Christians experience the Spirit at work, when they speak of a particular Bible verse "coming alive".

The Spirit delights to floodlight Jesus. For him to distract from Jesus would be self-contradictory. This means that any "spiritual" discovery or experience that doesn't make Jesus more real and more central is not from the Spirit of God.

The Spirit never does his own thing, but "speaks what he hears" from Christ (John 16:13). This all-inclusive task of the Spirit, leaving no place or purpose for blowing his own trumpet, reaches its finest expression in John 16:14: "He will bring glory to me." As York Minster is bathed in light each evening, on Jesus' glory the Holy Spirit always shines.

When our worship, our living and our thinking are inspired by the Holy Spirit, the one to be glorified will be Jesus Christ, and through him the Father. Like any truth of great value, this can be abused. Some distort it into an excuse to avoid thinking about the Spirit altogether: "The Spirit glorifies Christ, so let's consider Christ alone, and let the Spirit get on with his undercover work." This attitude falls down on two key points.

First, the New Testament avoids talking *only* about the Spirit, but confirms time and again that there is a clear and necessary place for direct teaching about him. This is seen above all in the brief but priceless teaching of Jesus on the Spirit.

Second, since the Spirit always glorifies Christ, the more our teaching about him fits the pattern of the New Testament, the more it will turn our eyes upon Jesus. Whenever the New Testament writers consider the Spirit, Jesus is floodlit and glorified.

These two principles cut the ground from under the

Spirit-avoiders. At the same time they serve as acid tests against the opposite excess of Spirit-infatuation.

Let's sum up the key discoveries of this chapter:

* Jesus is the man of the Spirit. He is our true role model and shows us how to live in the Spirit.

* Jesus is the Lord of the Spirit. He pours out upon us the power that makes the new life possible.

* The Holy Spirit has a floodlight ministry. He delights to bring glory neither to himself, nor to us, but to Christ alone.

Part Two

NEW LIFE IN THE SPIRIT

3

NEW BOLDNESS – THE SPIRIT OF EVANGELISM

Chapter one began with a mysterious "it". If "it" came into your life, you would naturally be apprehensive. We protect ourselves from such intrusion: "Keep off! This is *my* life!" We now have a much clearer idea of what the Spirit is like. And we have seen just how close the link is between Jesus and the Spirit. But we are still left with an awkward question: What will he want me to do? Or, even more uncomfortable, what will he do *to me*?

We will look at six great promises from the New Testament. First, Luke reveals new boldness in evangelism and new belonging with God and each other. Then we will see how Paul celebrates new confidence as sons and daughters of God, new holiness and new wholeness from the Spirit's life-changing power, and new harmony, as we learn to radiate God's love, living together in the Body of Christ.

Before turning to Luke, we have to make one thing clear, and it's not a very popular thought. The Old Testament revealed that God's Spirit is the source of all life and creativity. But the New Testament insists that the personal and permanent presence of the Spirit is only possible through Jesus.

The first Christians were convinced that they alone had entered the new age of the Spirit. They had been faithful Jews, but this new experience of God went way beyond anything they had known before.

This isn't arrogant. They aren't saying because we're such good people God has made his home with us. They don't pretend that they are better than anyone else. Instead they declare that because Jesus is Lord of the Spirit, only those who come to Jesus for forgiveness and a fresh start can possibly experience new life in the Spirit: "Salvation is found in no one else, for there is no other name under heaven given to men by which we must be saved" (Acts 4:12).

It's not that the Church is in control of the Spirit. Rather, the Church can only be Christ's Church when he pours out his Spirit in spiritual rebirth.

Many people don't like these exclusive claims. They want all religions and all good people to be inspired in exactly the same way. There is no room for this in the New Testament.

The first Christians were exclusive about the Spirit because they were exclusive about Jesus Christ: only through Jesus, salvation, only through Jesus, the gift of the Spirit. This exclusiveness was summed up by Jesus himself, when he taught about the Spirit: "The world cannot accept him, because it neither sees him nor knows him" (John 14:17).

A great chasm is fixed between the world and Jesus' followers. No one crosses the chasm by right of birth or by natural goodness. Jesus' followers aren't better people. They are simply those who have already accepted forgiveness on God's terms. Their responsibility to the world is immense: in their lives and words they carry the offer of life. In the words of Rebecca Manley Rippert, (*Out of the Saltshaker*, Leicester 1980): "The first Bible many people read will be your life."

Who's in charge here?

Witness to Jesus didn't begin at Pentecost. The Spirit had already been at work; testifying to Jesus is his special role, and only when the Spirit comes can the Christians join in his mission to the world. There's nothing wrong with planning and strategy, so long as God isn't left out until the last minute, and then invited to bless our bright ideas. Jesus wanted the Spirit to be in charge, and so the disciples had to sit and wait.

When he came he certainly made his presence felt. The

disciples might not have planned it that way, but their very first taste of the Spirit thrust them into the public eye. Almost before they knew it, they were into mass evangelism. Before follow-up or nurture groups were invented, there were 3,000 Christians. And this was their first day with the Spirit. No wonder Jesus had told them to wait.

The great commission directed the disciples to reach out in ever greater circles: "in Jerusalem, and in all Judea and Samaria, and then to the ends of the earth" (Acts 1:8). Luke emphasises that the Church of the Spirit fulfilled Jesus' command. First the gospel is proclaimed in Jerusalem (Acts 1:1–6:7) it spreads through Palestine and Samaria (Acts 6:8–9:31) and then it reaches Antioch (Acts 9:32–12:4). The second half of Acts records the spread of the gospel through Asia Minor (Acts 12:25–16:5), Europe (Acts 16:6–19:20) and finally to Rome (Acts 19:21–28:31).

In Jerusalem numbers swiftly rise from 3,000 to over 5,000 (Acts 4:4). Across the known world followers of The Way are baptised. In the power of the Spirit, Acts celebrates the supreme example of church growth.

Pentecost is a kind of preview. This one day anticipates the story that will unfold. Jews from many countries are gathered in Jerusalem for the festival. Later in Acts the gift of tongues will be used in worship without being overheard by outsiders. But at the beginning, all hear the mighty acts of God, declared "in our own tongues" (Acts 2:11).

Those who suggest that the disciples were simply speaking very clearly or very loudly deserve a special award for text evasion: if you don't like it, at all costs explain it away! Babel is reversed. There, city dwellers with a common language reached up to God in an absurd expression of human pride: a kind of prehistoric Manhattan to the nth degree. Here, city visitors with many different languages were each spoken to by God with the glorious gospel of Christ.

The task of the newborn Church is to witness to everyone. Jesus is for all mankind.

Spirit of surprises

The Spirit doesn't just bring results. He brings surprises. If he's in charge, Christians can expect the unpredictable.

When Philip evangelises the Samaritans, everything follows the familiar pattern. They express new found repentance and faith in Christ. They are baptised, but something is missing: the Spirit doesn't make his presence felt.

Only when apostles arrive from the Jerusalem HQ are the problems ironed out. Not until then does the Samaritan Pentecost completely parallel the Jerusalem experience.

Endless ink has been spilt over this event. Some say the Spirit is given to the Church, and can only be passed on through hands in the apostolic succession. That makes Acts 8 the first confirmation service. Others say the two stage experience is standard in a different way. The presence of the apostles is incidental, for the key element is the coming of the Spirit expressed by the gift of tongues.

Not surprisingly, the majority of commentators feel both these arguments push the evidence too far. If either was correct, all the other events in Acts need to be leant on hard to somehow fit the pattern.

The Samaritan Pentecost is *not* best explained by these two interpretations – the rite of confirmation or a mandatory second stage experience of the Spirit with mandatory tongues.

Most interpreters look instead to the ancient division between the Jews and the Samaritans. Both claimed to worship Yahweh, but as separate nations, with separate temples and priesthoods. Crossing into Samaria was the first critical expansion of the Christian Church. Would it retain its unity in the Spirit, or would it divide along the old national lines?

The Samaritans could have decided they were as much Christians as the converted (or completed) Jews. They could have set up the Samaritan Christian denomination. According to long established prejudices and mutual mistrust, this was not just possible but likely.

Luke records that God withheld the Spirit in a surprising way because an unexpected but crucial lesson had to be learned. For the Samaritans, it was the unmistakable discovery that they were part of the one new Church of Christ. They could not hang onto national independence and go it alone. For the Jews, on the authority of the eyewitness accounts of Peter and John, Samaritans had come into an identical experience of the Spirit. Jews could no longer claim national superiority, for all were equal in the one new people of God.

The second big surprise got even Peter into trouble. Cornelius was not only a Gentile, he was also a senior figure in the occupying army: a centurion in the Italian Regiment (Acts 10).

Peter knew quite clearly that some things were unclean, and it took the same dream three times over to prepare him for a triple shock:

"He saw heaven opened and something like a large sheet being let down to earth by its four corners. It contained all kinds of four-footed animals, as well as reptiles of the earth and birds of the air. Then a voice told him, 'Get up, Peter. Kill and eat.'

'Surely not, Lord!' Peter replied. 'I have never eaten anything impure or unclean.'

The voice spoke to him a second time, 'Do not call anything impure that God has made clean.'

This happened three times, and immediately the sheet was taken back to heaven" (Acts 10:11–16).

First he was invited to the house of the centurion Cornelius. Second, when he got there they asked for a sermon. Third, he had barely warmed to his theme when they began to talk. This wasn't Gentile rudeness, faced with the first overlong sermon: they were praying in tongues and praising God.

The dream had prepared him. His sermon spoke in theory about God having no favourites among the nations.

But Peter was still astonished. The Spirit didn't even wait for him to finish before bringing new life to the Gentiles: "Then Peter said, 'Can anyone keep these people from being baptised with water? They have received the Holy Spirit *just as we have*'" (Acts 10:46–7).

Predictably, the Jewish Christians were up in arms. As soon as possible they called a meeting and condemned Peter for entering a Gentile house and even eating with Gentiles.

Poor Peter was on the defensive. The ex-champion of ritual purity had to defend treating Gentiles as equals. He is careful to show it wasn't his idea. It was the Spirit who told him to go without delay, and the Spirit who gave him the dream. It was the Spirit who came upon the Gentiles, before Peter even considered baptising them. And the power of the Spirit was just like at Pentecost.

Some time later, the Church had to decide whether Jewish law should apply to Gentile Christians. Peter re-called the decisive miracle at Cornelius' house: "God, who knows the heart, showed that he accepted them by giving the Holy Spirit to them, just as he did to us. He made no distinction between us and them, for he purified their hearts by faith" (Acts 15:8–9).

The Spirit's coming on Cornelius made an unforgettable impression. God's plan was bigger than Jewish purity. The barriers of national pride and division were broken down.

The disciples had been slow to understand Jesus before his crucifixion. Even now the impact of the great com-mission was only just dawning. There would be no outer courts for Gentiles and inner courts for Jews in the new age. The message was relevant to all, and the promises were available to all.

If you are a Gentile reading this, be thankful. It is only because of the power of the Spirit that we are full members of the Christian Church. And if you are a Jewish Christian, it is because of the Spirit that we share in Christ that you can treat us not as inferiors, but equals, in the new Israel.

The Spirit was in charge, and the Spirit drew the Church

into evangelism. Being a Christian and bearing witness to Christ were inseparable. What's more, the Spirit was always unpredictable. He came in power and breathed new life where he wanted, not where men had planned. When it came to making Jesus' promises come true, the Spirit was several steps ahead of the Church. Times haven't changed.

It has been said that the "Church can live only by evangelising and by following wherever the Spirit leads." The Spirit in Acts is full of surprises, but never for their own sake. He is always spurring the Church on to fresh evangelism. He is never present just for kicks.

The Spirit is the lifeblood of the Church. Without the Spirit there could be no new community. But with the Spirit there always comes evangelism. Christian witness is not an occasional obligation for enthusiasts. It is the instinctive, normal and continual mark of the presence of the Spirit. To attempt to evangelise without the Spirit would be folly. To claim the Spirit for "my" experience, and leave evangelism to others was, for the first Christians, unthinkable.

Spirit of courage

The disciples were average men with an average lack of courage. When Christ was captured and crucified, the disciples fled. Their dreams were in tatters and their mouths were stopped. But Luke repeatedly emphasises a distinctive new quality after Pentecost. They don't whisper loyalty to Jesus in secret, behind locked doors. They proclaim the good news far and wide, "with boldness" and "with power". Peter and John were soon seized by the Jewish authorities. They were told in no uncertain terms to give up evangelism (Acts 4:1–17).

The response of the young Church is not to disband or become a secret society, but to pray. In their prayer they ask for a fresh filling of the Spirit. This is not to give them new peace of mind. Nor is it to protect them from arrest. Their first concern is not their own safety, but the unhindered proclamation of the gospel: "Enable your servants to speak your word with great boldness" (Acts 4:29).

Sure enough, when the Spirit comes, they are filled once more and all the believers "spoke the word of God boldly" (Acts 4:31). Again Peter and John are arrested. Again the Sanhedrin command them not to preach about Jesus. And again Peter and John claim their preaching comes from a higher authority.

They explain that the chief witness to Jesus is the Spirit. Because he witnesses and lives in them, they witness too. The Sanhedrin can command them all it likes, but they simply cannot give up evangelism. To do so would be to abandon God (Acts 5:32).

The end of Acts 5 confirms that this was no empty talk. "Day after day" the apostles preach. They preach in public in the temple courts. They preach in private from house to house. And day by day, despite all the threats, and despite what happened to Jesus so recently, new converts are added to the church.

If the Christians were surprised, the Jewish authorities were astonished. Other self-styled religious leaders had arisen in recent years. Some had been unmasked as frauds in their lifetime. Others had kept up appearances until death, but then their followers drifted away.

Jesus' disciples had lain low for the first few weeks after his death. The authorities must have hoped that the Galilean problem was already past history. But now they were back on the streets. Their courage was no flash in the pan. No threats could silence them.

The astonishment went even deeper. These men of new courage took on Jerusalem specialists in theological debate. They had a new understanding of the Old Testament and a new grasp of the promised Messiah. They claimed that Jesus who had taught them was God's own Son, raised by him from the dead, and now pouring out his Spirit.

Experience, theology and a new way of living all fitted together. They spoke with remarkable confidence and authority. But they were "unschooled, ordinary men". Unlettered fishermen simply didn't do that kind of thing!

Still worse, this new theological insight was combined with great clarity in preaching and popular appeal. Holding their own with the Jerusalem academics, the disciples of Jesus were on the same wavelength as the crowds. Few university types have ever been much good at mass communication. Yet the disciples were not experienced in this kind of speaking.

For courage and persistence, for clear insight and persuasive preaching, the disciples had the Sanhedrin bemused. It was just as Jesus had promised. The Spirit would come in power, he would give the right words to say, and he would glorify Jesus.

Signs and wonders

It wasn't just through new courage and new preaching that the Spirit witnessed to Jesus. At Pentecost, the miraculous gift of tongues drew an enormous crowd, and led to the conversion of 3,000. A little while later, Peter and John are stopped at the Beautiful Gate to the Temple by a man crippled from birth (Acts 3). They have no money to offer him, but they heal him in Jesus' name. Once more a crowd gathers, Peter preaches, and the church grows to 5,000.

Where the Spirit is at work, all kinds of people can see the difference. They start asking questions, and evangelistic preaching provides the answers. The Spirit causes the event, draws the crowd and inspires the explanation. And in all of this he glorifies Jesus.

Signs and wonders were not freakish or fringe activities for the first church. When they prayed for the Spirit to give boldness in preaching, they also prayed for miracles. "Stretch out your hand to heal and perform miraculous signs and wonders through the name of your holy servant Jesus" (Acts 4:30). Sure enough, just as the Spirit gave them boldness he provided miracles.

Acts 5 tells of many signs and wonders among the Christians. They gathered regularly at Solomon's colonnade, and crowds gathered too, bringing their sick to be healed.

These miracles were not the latest gimmick to draw a crowd. They were genuine expressions of the love of God. Just as Jesus had healed out of pure love, there is no suggestion that the disciples only prayed for healing for those already converted. Nor is it ever suggested that miracles were simply a means of producing "conversion fodder".

The great desire of the first Christians was to see many others receive forgiveness and enter the new age of the Spirit through the death and resurrection of Christ. The signs and wonders expressed directly the love of God for women and men.

When the Church neglects an aspect of the New Testament, we begin to edit those verses out of our reading or preaching. We begin to act as if they don't exist. Stephen is remembered by many as the first Christian martyr and one of the first deacons (Acts 6). He was a great preacher, and when the authorities seized him, he preached a heroic martyr's sermon. All of this is quite well known.

Less well known is that Luke stresses Stephen was "full of faith and of the Holy Spirit" (Acts 6:5). Verse eight of chapter six is often passed over as if it didn't exist: "Now Stephen, a man full of God's grace and power, *did great wonders and miraculous signs among the people.*"

It wasn't just the apostles. A deacon was involved as well. His was no mere administrative post on the church fabric committee. Signs and wonders were the common fare of the Jerusalem Church. As J. B. Phillips wrote in the introduction to his book *The Young Church in Action* (London 1955): "They did not hold conferences on psychosomatic medicine; they simply healed the sick."

Full of the Spirit in his preaching and full of the Spirit in his signs and wonders, Stephen is full of the Spirit again at the moment of martyrdom. It is then that he receives his final vision in this life of "Jesus standing at the right hand of God" (Acts 7:55).

Once more the Spirit is true to himself and his task. He inspires Stephen in great danger to bear witness to Jesus, and in the vision he confirms that Jesus is glorified.

As the Church spread, signs and wonders spread with it. Paul refers frequently in his letters to "signs following". Luke confirms this in Acts 14. Paul and Barnabas preach at Iconium, and make a good impression on both Jews and Gentiles. But those Jews who reject the message stir up opposition.

As at Jerusalem, instead of going underground to save their own skins, the Christians are inspired by the Spirit to "speak boldly for the Lord". Their testimony is more than courageous words. Luke has shown how signs and wonders can gather a crowd. Now he confirms that they can also follow preaching, authenticating in dramatic experience the presence of God and the Gospel of grace: ". . . the Lord . . . confirmed the message of his grace by enabling them to do miraculous signs and wonders" (Acts 14:3).

Signs and wonders don't just declare the love of God and confirm the message of Christ. They also prevent the Church becoming racist or sectarian. In Acts 15 the Church has reached a crisis. As numbers grow, and more Gentiles are converted, the original Jewish Christians have to decide whether the Gentiles are their equals in Christ, or whether they still need to be circumcised and come under the law of Israel.

Two key contributions to the debate come from Peter and Paul. They do not concentrate on theological principle or human initiative. Instead, they describe the surprising acts of the Spirit.

Peter cites the gift of the Spirit to Cornelius; that persuaded him God "made no distinction between us and them" (Acts 15:9).

When Paul and Barnabas speak, the whole assembly is silenced. They don't concentrate on examples of individual Gentile conversions. Instead they confirm that the gospel of Christ is for all by telling of their missionary experiences.

They don't have slides to project or samples of Gentile handicraft, but they can tell of something more vivid and memorable. God has been at work. And his method, just like at Jerusalem, has been to use signs and wonders: "The whole assembly became silent as they listened to Barnabas and Paul telling about the miraculous signs and wonders God had done among the Gentiles through them" (Acts 15:12).

This power is both exciting and awesome. Simon the sorcerer knew his own trickery was no match for it (Acts 8:9–24). Such power was enviable, and could be the means to much money and fame. He did as any charlatan would, and tried to buy the Spirit from Peter. He made a double mistake. No man controls the Spirit of God, not even the apostles. What's more, the Spirit is only given by God to those who repent and are baptised into Christ. The power of the Spirit always glorifies Jesus. The Spirit is never fuel for profit in a commercial enterprise. The Spirit is never for sale.

While Peter ruled out any attempt to exploit the Spirit for personal gain, Stephen gave a warning to those who reject the gospel. To reject the message is to resist the Spirit. To resist the Spirit is to reject God (Acts 7).

Signs and wonders aren't important in Acts just for evangelism, but that is their central thrust. Signs and wonders aren't a necessary part of every evangelistic activity, but they are remarkably frequent in the early Church. They aren't caused by human faith, but they are God's gifts of love to his needy church. Through the presence and power of the Spirit, signs and wonders glorify Jesus as Lord.

It would be quite easy to overstate the role of signs and wonders in the New Testament. But for most of us that is not a pressing problem. Instead, we read the Bible as if they didn't exist.

Faced with signs and wonders in the early Church we must ask uncomfortable questions. Is our reading of the

New Testament selective? Do we pick and choose those activities of the Spirit we approve, and ignore the rest? If we do, we risk rejecting not just those activities but the Spirit, and in resisting him we resist God.

The Jerusalem Church left the Jewish authorities with a big problem. Everyone in Jerusalem knew about the healing of the cripple at the Beautiful Gate. (Acts 4:16). Signs and wonders were hot news which backed up the claim to new life in Christ.

The opponents of the Christians couldn't deny they had remarkable power. Many didn't understand the new age of the Spirit, but they could see its results with their own eyes. They didn't have to ask, "What difference does it make if you become a Christian?" Instead they asked, "How do you explain these life-changes and miracles that everyone can see?"

Paul's mission in the Spirit

The second half of Acts concentrates on Paul. Luke doesn't lose for a moment his stress on the Spirit. Struck blind by the vision of Jesus on the Damascus Road, Paul was commanded to wait in the city for instructions.

Poor Ananias. He knew all about Paul, one of the worst persecutors who had gone head-hunting for Christians. Now Ananias was told in prayer to go and visit him. He must have taken some convincing.

In the end he came. He repeated the words given by the Spirit, commissioning Paul to be an evangelist to the Gentiles. As the Spirit filled Paul, "something like scales fell from [his] eyes, and he could see again." (Acts 9:18) Paul had thought he was serving God by persecuting Christians. When the Spirit came, he could at last see clearly that to serve God meant to proclaim Jesus as Lord and Saviour.

Luke is at pains to stress the crucial role of the Spirit at the beginning of Paul's Christian life. But that is by no means the last word. While the church at Antioch was worshipping and fasting, they decided to set aside two of their key leaders for out-of-town missions. This wasn't a human proposal to the church meeting, or the decision of the elders. Instead, the one who spoke, through prophecy, was the Holy Spirit (Acts 13:2).

The same Spirit stays involved on Paul's journeys. It is the Spirit who keeps him from preaching in Asia (Acts 16:6). It is the Spirit who compels him to go to Jerusalem (Acts 20:22). It is the Spirit who warns him "in every city" of the "prison and hardships" to be faced at Jerusalem (Acts 20:23). And it is the Spirit through the prophet Agabus who reveals that the Jews will bind Paul and hand him over to the Romans for trial (Acts 21:11–13).

The Spirit doesn't only guide, he warns of trouble to come. But Paul never takes the easy way out. He accepts that the presence of the Spirit is not to preserve his own skin. Instead, the presence of the Spirit invites, equips and requires him to be devoted to his particular God-given task – "testifying to the gospel of God's grace" (Acts 20:24).

The presence of the Spirit is an acid test of true conversion. We might ask, "Have you received Jesus?" or "Have you been born again?". When Paul meets some followers of John the Baptist from Ephesus he asks, "Did you receive the Holy Spirit when you believed?" (Acts 19:2).

It's not that Paul wants all Christians to go through a mandatory second stage of conversion. It's not that he wants everyone to have carbon copies of his own experience. What he does recognise is that the presence of the Spirit is the hallmark of *every* true Christian.

There are two reasons that make us sure of Paul's meaning. First, the Ephesians reply they didn't even know there was a Holy Spirit. Their understanding is as deficient as their faith. Like making new year resolutions they had repented of the past. But they have no confidence in forgiveness, no new encounter with God, and no new inner power for future change. Repentance on its own is not the full gospel of Jesus Christ.

Second, Paul teaches them not only about the Spirit but

about the need to believe in Christ. He takes them right back to basics. And then he baptises them. This is most important, because it is the only time in Acts when people are "rebaptised".

Paul is quite clear that John's baptism is not enough. It is not the same as Christian baptism. All Christians need to be baptised not just for repentance, but to be baptised into Christ and to be baptised with the Holy Spirit. The Spirit is essential for every believer.

All Christian churches recognise the importance of baptism. But the new reality of the Spirit has often been underplayed. Just imagine the fuss if Paul asked nominal churchgoers today, "Did you receive the Spirit when you believed?"

Christians are sometimes known as *the people who don't* . . . don't drink . . . don't smoke . . . don't smile . . . don't know how to have fun. In Acts, the Christians are more alive than ever they were before. Paul simply couldn't see that positive Christian difference in the Ephesians, and so he asked about the Spirit. We need to ask whether our non-Christian friends can see the positive difference in us.

The Ephesians replied they didn't know the Spirit existed. Once I would have had to reply, "Well, Paul, I know there is a Spirit, but I'd rather talk about something else." We act as if the Spirit was not a suitable subject for polite Christian company. Nothing in the New Testament can possibly justify our avoidance of the Spirit of God.

Every Christian a witness

Hardly anything happens in Acts without Luke stressing the Spirit was in charge. Paul's testimony is recorded three times and always combines two things: the objective offer of a fresh beginning through the historical death and resurrection of Jesus, and also Paul's subjective experience of a life being changed in the Spirit. Revealed truth and personal experience come together as the vital heart of all fully Christian testimony.

Not all the first Christians were great evangelists. Luke concentrates on Peter and Paul, but he never suggests this is the only way God works. In Acts chapter eight, the ordinary Christians prove just as courageous. After Stephen's martyrdom, the Jerusalem Church is scattered under fierce persecution. But the believers did not go underground to protect themselves. Instead, they "preached the word wherever they went" (Acts 8:4).

Not all are called to be Billy Grahams. But the Spirit enables all to be faithful witnesses to Christ, in both life and words. According to Luke this can be difficult, and yet quite natural. Changed lives will be noticed. People will ask for explanations.

I remember someone asking, "Shouldn't we keep it from non-Christians when we feel down?" That reduces witness to soap-sud advertising. Christ is "sold" for providing the best feelings, like a superior grade of "happiness pill". That was not what set the early church on fire.

The Spirit is the Spirit of Truth, pointing to what Jesus has already done. He is also the Spirit of deep inner change, sometimes dramatic and sudden, sometimes painfully slow. We need to learn our evangelism from the New Testament, not from TV slogans. Jesus promised the truth would set us free.

Luke records open air meetings and organised debates. There is witness in public and witness in homes. Chance meetings on journeys become opportunities for evangelism. Reputation leads to invitations to speak out for Christ. Even arrest can lead to more people hearing the gospel.

The new age of the Spirit is marked by the desire to proclaim the gospel. There is no single technique or method for every Christian and every situation. But all are called, in many different ways, to "testify to the grace of Christ".

You cannot be a Christian without receiving the Spirit. You cannot be truly open to the Spirit without being ready and willing to be active in evangelism. The Spirit never distracts from Christian mission to a needy world. In fact he promotes it. The age of the Spirit is the age of evangelism.

4

NEW BELONGING

Evangelism is vital. But it can never be the whole work of the Spirit. A church that did nothing but evangelise would be very boring. Evangelism would turn the body of Christ into an arm ever reaching out to draw new people in. Once they join up, they find there is no body behind the arm. They simply have to become part of it, grabbing new people to become part of the grabbing arm, who grab yet more people . . .

No church is quite like that. But just as some relegate evangelism to a once every few years duty, others give little help with post-conversion growth. Jesus didn't send out the disciples to make nominal converts for pew sitting or growth statistics. His command was to make disciples.

Evangelism is the main theme of Acts. But Luke doesn't suggest for one moment that evangelism is the only task of the Church, or that if you are thoroughly involved with evangelism, you have nothing more to receive from the Spirit.

Even before the mission begins, Luke makes two things quite clear. The Spirit brings a new closeness to God, through what Jesus has done for us. And the Spirit brings a new closeness between those who have entered the new family of Christ.

Spirit of worship

When the Spirit came at Pentecost, the disciples were sitting down. Luke stresses this because the normal Jewish postures for prayer were standing or kneeling. The new age didn't come as a reward for men's faithfulness. It came as a surprise, and confirmed that God was in control of his Church.

Soon evangelism would begin with Peter's magnificent sermon. But the first thing the Spirit caused was new worship. The crowds outside made no mistake – "we hear them declaring the wonders of God in our own tongues" (Acts 2:11).

Worship is the first calling of humankind, and the first priority of the Christian. Worship as the disciples had never known it before was the first gift from the Spirit. Worship became the hallmark of the new church.

The first Christians *"praised God* and enjoyed the favour of all people" (Acts 2:47). The healed cripple was walking and leaping and *praising God* (Acts 3:8). All the people were *praising God* for signs and wonders (Acts 4:21). When Cornelius and his household received the Spirit they *praised God* (Acts 10:46). When the Jewish Christians saw that Gentiles could be filled with the Spirit they *praised God* (Acts 11:18; 21:20).

Worship marked the birth of the Church. It shaped their meetings and their everyday life. We have seen how the Jerusalem church prayed for boldness when the Jewish authorities tried to ban evangelism. Even then, faced with dark threats of imprisonment or death, the first half of their prayer is devoted to adoration and thanksgiving. We saw their prayer answered by new boldness in mission. Even before that, it is answered by new boldness in worship.

Praise of God leads to a new filling with the Spirit, which in turn inspires still further praise and adoration. As the Christians praise God for what he has done, they also anticipate what he will do when Jesus comes again. Between those two certainties God has not withdrawn himself. They remain open and expectant for what God will give *today*. If our worship squeezes out the presence of God today, if there is no room in our worship for surprises of the Spirit, then we have drifted badly from the worship of the New Testament.

In Acts 4 it wasn't simply that they enjoyed worship

together, and so called that a fresh filling of the Spirit. They felt a real difference from the dramatic coming of God. The room where they were actually shook. And their worship entered a new dimension.

I remember once in particular when a similar thing happened. A crowd of about one hundred were enjoying a quiet and gentle time of worship. Suddenly everything was different. The room didn't shake. But the presence of God became real in a new way. No one wanted to leave. There was no need to explain anything. The Lord was inhabiting the praises of his people, and we knew it.

No ordinary experience or emotional high comes anywhere near the reality of the glory of God: "we have confidence to enter the Most Holy Place by the blood of Jesus" (Heb 10:19).

Worship is not centred on *my* feelings. If you join in worship for the sake of an emotional afterglow, true worship has been betrayed. Worship in the Spirit is centred on the glory, majesty and holiness of God, and on his mighty acts in history, supremely in the gift of his Son.

But true worship is always more than dry repetition of doctrines and facts. Cold conformity to a set of beliefs kills an attitude of praise. Just as the Spirit is personal, true worship is fully personal. It should never be like pledging allegiance to the flag or reciting the boy scout or girl guide law. True worship expresses and experiences relationship with God. That is the highest calling for any Christian.

Once we've established that emotional highs are not the reason or purpose of worship, we need to hear Luke emphasise the reality of Christian joy. As the Spirit inspires us to worship, he fills us with joy. Joy is so much the hallmark of the Spirit, Luke links them together time and again.

Peter claims a new fulfilment of David's words – "you fill me with your presence" (Acts 2:28). In Samaria, healings and exorcisms lead to "great joy in the city" (Acts 8:8). Even under persecution at Pisidian Antioch, the disciples are filled with the Holy Spirit and with joy (Acts 13:52).

When Paul's jailer and his family are converted, all of them are filled with joy (Acts 16:34). The Ethiopian eunuch who was baptised near the Gaza Road by Philip never sees the evangelist again, but now the Spirit has filled him, and he "went on his way rejoicing" (Acts 8:39).

Worship is open to the Spirit's leading. Worship is centred on what God has done in Christ. Worship builds up the Church and has direct evangelistic impact. Worship brings a dramatic sense of the presence of God in a new experience of joy. But Luke has still more to say.

First, worship is not restricted to particular buildings at particular times in the week. In the new age the Spirit fills the believers, not the Temple. The presence of the Spirit, the new relationship with God and the new kind of worship are not tacked onto life as something extra. Paul at Athens explains, "in him we live and move and have our being" (Acts 17:28).

Relationship with God is at the heart of the new life. The Spirit's presence is all-inclusive. He is concerned to take charge of the whole of life, not just the religious bits.

Deep sea diving takes people briefly into a new environment. Without oxygen cylinders life there is not possible for us. Without the Spirit, the new dimension of worship and joy is not available. But with the Spirit, no part of life need ever be quite the same.

It would, of course, be possible to walk around on dry land dressed in all the equipment of a deep sea diver. Those who receive the Spirit may then ignore him, put up a sign on their lives saying "business as usual", and only relate to God for an hour on Sundays. That was not the life in the Spirit which caused such a stir in the Roman Empire.

Only the Spirit can free us from deep rooted conformity to our own culture and age. We need to cultivate an inclusive and integrated Christian life, open to be filled in every part. That will make the church in the eyes of outsiders more relevant, less "religious" and probably more attractive.

Second, Luke emphasises a memorable phrase in Peter's

second sermon. Peter calls for repentance and turning to God, that "times of refreshing may come from the Lord" (Acts 3:19). Once more, worship is a relationship to be experienced, not a concept to be codified. Once more, language of emotion is used.

I used to avoid this kind of promise. While the psalmist rejoiced on the way to God's house (Ps 122:1), I rejoiced in my head, but not often in my heart. I was strong on theory, but weak on relationship.

I still remember the breakthrough of going to a church where worship was lively, relevant and real. Open to the Spirit in new ways, I found myself hurrying to get to Sunday services. The psalmist, I realised, was talking from his experience, not from cold theory.

For Peter, "times of refreshing from the Lord" wasn't some kind of fancy high-flown language, dressing up everyday religion. The Holy Spirit was a living reality. Worship isn't the place to add starch to a stiff upper lip, but the place where God is met.

Peter's words are a promise to meditate on. We may need refreshing from tiredness or overwork. Worship may have grown dull and prayer stale. Our faith may have lost its zest and cutting edge.

"Times of refreshing" are the gift of God's Spirit. They don't come by being more religious, by self-improvement, or by extra Christian activities. The Spirit is with us, and through worship in song, words and silence he can make his presence known (Ps 22:26). With healing on his wings he brings peace. James said, "Draw near to God, and he will draw near to you." (Jas 4:8).

For some this kind of meditative prayer comes naturally. But most of us in the modern world are too rushed and too busy to relax easily into the presence of God. Isaiah speaks of perfect peace given to those whose "mind is stayed" or "centred down" on God (Isa 26:3). It is not easy to stop our minds racing: but it is immeasurably worthwhile. Richard Foster suggests you hold out your hands, palms down, and let go of those anxieties and cares that make your mind race and your heart distant from God. Name them before him, and as you let them go centre your mind on God and become open once more to his presence.

The promise of "times of refreshing" is not just for the prayer specialists and the naturally peaceful types. Those who are overbusy need most of all to step aside from the rush. The Spirit is available to all Christians. And through his presence, every single Christian is invited to experience "times of refreshing" and God's "perfect peace".

New Family

The Spirit could have come privately. He could have baptised each disciple at home, when they were ready. Instead he came on the first 12 at the same time, when they were all together.

At Pentecost the Spirit made two things quite clear: without individual faith in Christ, the Spirit won't come at all; but when he does come, the individual is no longer alone. The Spirit baptises each of us into the one new Family of Christ.

The first Christians were a mixed bunch, but they all had one thing in common: the Spirit. And the Spirit was beginning to develop a family likeness and a new sense of belonging.

I remember a TV series in which a pretty girl in her late teens had just moved to Manhattan from Grand Rapids, Michigan. A quiet provincial community was replaced by the buzz of the Big Apple. She didn't know how to settle or what to do.

One of the born and bred New Yorkers took her in hand. When riding the subway or on the sidewalk, she had always to remember the three keeps. Keep your eyes to yourself. Keep your voice to yourself. And keep your money out of sight. It would be like living in her own private world. Big Apple survival was based on strict isolation and anonymity.

A few years ago I saw a newspaper photo of a New York bar. On the floor lay a corpse, felled by a heart attack. With their backs to him, the regulars still propped up the bar. There was nothing they could do to help, so why let a dead man disturb their drinking!

It's not just the down and outs. More recently an American TV broadcaster was mugged outside his expensive apartment block. It was generally a safe part of the city. He was well known. But no one offered help for some twelve hours. They left him in the gutter, bruised and beaten in his dinner jacket. City life says it's safer not to care.

It's not just New York. And it's not just the States. As life gets faster, "home" is no longer a community. It's only the place you sleep. I recently met a family where the grandparents had moved once in over fifty years of marriage. The parents averaged seven years in each home. But the third generation had averaged two years per home in the first eight years of marriage. They hadn't rented camels and a nomad's tent. They reflect the typical experience of the last three generations.

The average stay of a graduate in a first job is under three years. In urban areas, friends are drawn from work and leisure pursuits. You don't walk near your home, but you get straight into the car. You may nod to neighbours, but you rarely get to know them.

Once people belonged to a local community. Some no doubt felt trapped. But for most it was a supportive and enduring network of family and friends. Today when you ask, "Where are you from?" an increasing number say they don't really know.

Families are dispersed over countries and continents. Young parents don't have the back-up of grannies or other relatives. More and more singles are living alone. A community is not much more than an address, and family are too distant to help out as they once did.

We are an uprooted age. Everyone's on the move. The most common problem today isn't money or sex. It's loneliness.

Proud independence distorts our reading of the Bible.

We can see clearly the need for personal faith and commitment. We can see salvation has nothing to do with pedigree and cannot be inherited. But if someone talks about "group identity" we soon get uncomfortable. Everyone warns about peer pressure or shallow conformity, and so we risk missing out on becoming the church *together*.

Isolation is mirrored in the drive-in church. The British smile in a superior way at such strange novelties. But some Christians go to walk-in churches in the same style. You park your car outside, but you might just as well still be in it. You sit separately in your regular pew, and I sit in mine. If we really cannot avoid speaking to someone, it is kept to the traditional non-conversation: How are you? Fine thanks, and you?

The victims of isolation aren't noticed. They carry their loneliness into church with them. They sit alone in a pew. Then an hour later they carry their secret burden home.

Clubs are the common comfort of suburbanites. Clubs are where like-minded people from similar backgrounds get together. If you can't see the appeal of aerobics or folk dancing, or you are not the right sort, there's no place in the club for you.

For the insiders, clubs are a great success. They work well and are all to the good. But then you get clubby churches. You can soon tell if you don't belong. It might be the accent or the way you dress. They may require the presence of certain key phrases or the absence of certain pastimes. In a club church, people are united first by what they already have in common – their accents, backgrounds and jobs. Christians who don't fit don't stay.

In the first Church, the one thing in common was Christ. The Spirit in all believers united them in one family. Being a family wasn't easy, but it was in a different league to being a club. They really belonged and they really cared.

The Spirit gave this liberation. The believers felt more at home, more wanted and welcome than they had ever felt before. If they had "kept themselves to themselves" they wouldn't just have elbowed other Christians to a clubland distance. They would have elbowed out the Spirit too.

The new family of the age of the Spirit is summed up by Luke: "All the believers were one in heart and mind" (Acts 4:32). They didn't all speak identical words, or think identical thoughts. The Spirit didn't bring the heartless sameness of some modern cults. He didn't crush individuality as it seemed to be crushed in the boiler-suited millions of Mao's China. There was room in the one Church for people as different as James the practical, John the reflective and Peter the impulsive. Soon there would be room for Paul the ex-persecutor too.

The new Church was united but not uniform. The Spirit enriched each unique individual, and at the same time he inspired new acceptance of each other. The prophecy from Joel which Peter quoted at Pentecost stressed that the one Spirit came for many different kinds of people: sons and daughters will prophesy, the Spirit will be poured out on both men and women, young men will see visions and old men will dream dreams. The Spirit didn't just inspire the apostles, who then drew others together. The one Spirit was and is for *everybody*.

All ages, all races, all types, all could be accepted and drawn together. The laws of class and clubland are broken. All Christians are free to be family. No one is left out.

You can feel it in some churches. There is a spirit of acceptance and belonging as soon as you walk through the door. People who would have little in common without Christ now live together in his love. Of course it needs working at. It is sometimes much easier to stick with your own age group or type. And a Church that is truly a family will be a magnet for the needy people who find it hard to cope.

But what if the generations are at odds with each other? What if some sing half-heartedly any old-fashioned hymn, and others sit tight-lipped through anything modern? What if jeans always sit separately from jackets and ties? All of us need to look long and hard at the New Testament vision of the Church.

In Christ the dividing wall is broken down. The Spirit is devoted to reconciling opposites. He will never crush individuality. But a new family is both his promise and his demand.

Acts 2:42–7 presents Luke's vision for the Church. It has stirred and captured the imaginations of Christians ever since. This is what the Church can be. This is what the Church is meant to be:

> They devoted themselves to the apostles' teaching and to the fellowship, to the breaking of bread and to prayer. Everyone was filled with awe, and many wonders and miraculous signs were done by the apostles. All the believers were together and had everything in common. Selling their possessions and goods, they gave to anyone as he had need. Every day they continued to meet together in the temple courts. They broke bread in their homes and ate together with glad and sincere hearts, praising God and enjoying the favour of all the people. And the Lord added to their number daily those who were being saved.

Luke is not being impossible. This is no romantic idealism. He is quite frank about the failures of the first church. There is personal disagreement, racial pride, and temporary neglect of the needy. The apostles become overworked, and have to learn about team ministry and delegation.

This healthy realism makes the vision still more relevant. The problems and flaws of the first Christians weren't hidden away from public view. But that didn't blur their priorities or shrivel their faith. They didn't become disillusioned or feel stuck with second best.

The Church didn't start on a spiritual high only to slide inevitably downhill ever since. Those who believe in the Spirit need also to believe in the Church. The Church is the Spirit's gift to every believer.

Four priceless activities released God's glory in the
Jerusalem Church: teaching, fellowship, breaking of bread
and prayer. Teaching because God has spoken, and his
word is always relevant and needed. Fellowship because
the new family needs working at – "All men will know that
you are my disciples, if you love one another" (John 13:35).
Breaking of bread because Christ gave this meal to his
Church, to remember his sacrifice, once-for-all, to feed on
him by faith in our hearts today, and to anticipate the great
bridal feast when he comes again. And prayer, because
without regular communication, as individuals and
together, a living relationship freezes into frigid formality.

It really is no surprise that the Jerusalem Church grew
every day. They had no desire to be an exclusive and inward
looking club for religious specialists. Empowered by his
Spirit they were the new family of God.

Luke's message is plain: for the Church to be renewed,
the Spirit must be in charge. Where the Spirit is in charge,
all four of these priorities need attention. None are optional. Yet it is so easy for the other activities in a local
church to drain the lion's share of our time and energy.
With this quartet in harmony, the family can flourish, new
converts are added, and God's glory is in the Church. When
they are neglected, faith shrivels and discord reigns.

When J. B. Phillips translated the Book of Acts, he said
he felt in these pages "the fresh air of heaven plainly
blowing":

> . . . the Spirit of God found what surely he must always be
> seeking – a fellowship of men and women so united in
> love and faith that he can work in them and through them
> with the minimum of let and hindrance. Consequently it
> is a matter of sober historical fact that never before
> has any small body of ordinary people so moved the
> world that their enemies could say, with tears of rage in
> their eyes, that these men "have turned the world
> upside down" (*The Young Church in Action*, London
> 1955).

New community

All lonely people are offered a new family in the Spirit. All who store up treasure on earth are offered instead treasure in heaven. The first Church encouraged a radical break with materialism, as well as proud isolation.

The new family didn't just love with emotions and with time. They loved with possessions until it hurt. This wasn't early communism. Peter stressed to Ananias and Sapphira that their possessions were their own. What they did with them was between themselves and God. The apostles never commandeered a new convert's wealth. But the community came to matter more to individuals than their personal taste for luxuries.

This release from materialism is expressed in two ways. First, the Christians were freed by the Spirit from possessiveness. The child of God didn't need to measure status in terms of *my* belongings or *my* lifestyle. Each had received the unsearchable riches of Christ.

Second, the Spirit gave a new recognition of equality. Because the Spirit had come equally on all, none could claim the right to material indulgence while others in the family were in need. Jesus didn't come to provide new laws, he came to deal with people. To turn from the prompting of the Spirit to legal sanction in the Church would mean turning from communalism, where fellowship matters more than wealth, into communism, where enforced equality crushes freedom. When the Spirit enriched human freedom, no one in the church was left needy.

Some try to argue that the Jerusalem Church was fanatical. Because they pooled all their goods, the argument goes, they went bankrupt, and other churches had to bail them out. We have to be careful. There is no direct or necessary link between Acts chapter two and the later problems at Jerusalem. What's more, although Luke gives very little detail about the everyday life of the Church, he stresses voluntary community by describing it twice:

All the believers were together and had everything in common. Selling their possessions and goods, they gave to anyone as they had need (Acts 2:44–5).

All the believers were one in heart and mind. No one claimed that any of his possessions was his own, but they shared everything they had . . . There was no needy person among them (Acts 4:32,34).

For Luke, this is by no means the first grave error of the Church. It is the natural and spontaneous result of being the new community of Christ. In a materialistic age, it was an astonishing testimony to the Spirit's transforming power.

We should let these verses trouble us, rather than speedily evade them. Before we dismiss them we need to hear three things: the warning of Jesus, the invitation of the Spirit and the cry of the poor.

Treasure on earth

I believe we can only understand the radical freedom of the first Christian community by looking at Jesus' teaching on earthly treasures in the Sermon on the Mount. Jesus' teaching was surely the driving force behind the church as the new community of love. In the power of the Spirit, Jesus is the inspiration for their new way of living.

When Jesus talks about money, materialism and the way we live, we know we are all in trouble! In Matthew chapter six there are two main themes, money and worry. This is no accident, and gives us our first principle about treasure on earth.

1 Love of money always brings worry
Money, it has been said, is made round to slip through your fingers. When money speaks, truth is silent. It can buy you everything except happiness, and pay your fare to every place except heaven. Naturally most of us hate a lot of money . . . when someone else is spending it. A Texas

multi-millionaire said, "If it don't make money, it ain't pretty." Jesus said not money itself but the love of money is the root of all evil. Most of us know something about that love.

Jesus highlights the inevitable threats to treasure on earth – moths, rust and thieves. Most of us do indeed worry whether what we have is safe. We worry about our food and clothes, our homes and our savings. If we don't worry about having any food and clothes, we worry about having the finest food and the most fashionable clothes. The love of money always brings worry.

2 Where money rules there is never enough

Jesus talks about storing up treasure on earth, stockpiling more and more and waiting for happiness. Do you have a big enough house? Is your interest rate high enough? The catch word is *enough*. Enough is never enough.

All our energy can be devoted to having one new possession. I remember when the new Ford Escort came out. There was a dealer near our home, and all we wanted was a Ford Escort. Eventually we bought one, and were quite the proudest of owners. But within a few months they brought out new styling. Then we began to look at larger models. Satisfaction is always around the corner that never comes.

Money holds out fulfilment tomorrow, but there's always something else to buy. "Once we're settled in we'll begin to give more money." But then the car goes wrong, or you need new curtains. Seneca described the consumer society when he said, "The most grievous kind of destitution is to want money in the midst of wealth." Money is like salt water. The more you drink, the thirstier you become.

3 Money always promises more than it delivers

As Jesus said, if moths, rust and thieves don't catch up with you, death will. Love of money destroys our true dignity. It reduces us from people to consumers.

A friend of ours was interviewed for a job. – "What do you want from life in ten years time?" The only answer they were interested in was salary. Carlyle said, "For every hundred men who can stand adversity, there is only one who can stand prosperity."

Did you see the long BBC interview with Richard Burton which was rebroadcast when he died? The greatest actor of his generation was reduced to making bad films for big money. I think he said that one year he earned £7 million, and spent it. Near the end of the programme he said something like this: "I don't trust people. I can count on the fingers of one hand the people I trust."

Money promised happiness and fulfilment. The main things it delivered were loneliness, cynicism, and the need for more money.

4 Nothing that is God's can be bought for money

Acts 8 tells of Simon the sorcerer who tried to buy the Holy Spirit from Peter and John. Peter explained that salvation is not for sale.

When Jesus met the rich young ruler, he saw he was caught in the net of love of money. That man's love of money was so strong, the only way out was to sell all he had and give to the poor. Jesus didn't give that advice to everyone, but he gave it when it was needed.

We need to reflect on the rich young ruler. He didn't have many of the possessions that all of us in the West call necessities. But he was trapped by what he had. Money promises to make you special, but the price can be your freedom.

Jesus provides home truths about love of money. This doesn't mean that TVs or videos or hi-fis are wrong. We should thank God for them and be grateful. But we need to recognise that our money and our love of money make severe demands upon us. According to Jesus, our lifestyle is dangerous. Treasure on earth can be terminal for spiritual health.

The web of materialism

Jesus summed up treasure on earth like this: "the pagans run after all these things" (Matt 6.32). We need to look hard at our everyday materialism in the light of his warning.

Materialism makes the world go around. It is the blood in the veins of a selfish society. Materialism is not just having possessions. It's a way of life and a complete set of values.

Our culture is built on the latest, the most modern, the disposable. First it was new bathrooms. Then new kitchens. Tomorrow it will be TVs with built in video and computer.

Advertising tells us not only what's latest, but that without the latest we're not happy. We won't be loved. We're so out of touch we're positively prehistoric. Or, perhaps worst of all, without the latest we must be depriving the children.

Wherever we turn materialism is selling its wares. Radio and TV, magazines, sport and billboards. The new gadgets in friends' houses beckon us to buy even better.

We are a society built on instant credit and instant consumption. Buy now and regret it when the monthly payments come through. All the free newspapers that come tumbling through our doors each week declare there's always someone somewhere ready to sell something to you. Until you read the advert, you didn't even know your life was incomplete without it.

But materialism isn't just an up to the minute silicon chip driven merry-go-round. It has five profoundly destructive consequences.

1 Materialism leaves out God
Life is too busy. All energies are channelled into getting on and getting more. We replace knowledge of God by tele-text. We don't pray before we buy; we pay by credit card. We shift from practising the presence of God to sound all round. God is kept to the religious bits only. A hobby for Sunday mornings.

2 Materialism rejects the poor

At the 1984 Republican Convention, a man worth forty million dollars had doubled his "value" in President Reagan's first term. He was particularly in favour of tax cuts for the rich. Meantime the poor in the States have got poorer.

Still worse, the poor in the two-thirds world are getting less and less of the total world's wealth. We buy their resources cheap. We destroy or hoard our food surplus to keep prices high. We sell them more tanks than useful equipment. Shirley Williams has recently noted that the new genetically manipulated plants are being developed for growth in the rich north. The south won't even have their cash crops to sell us.

The Brandt Report recognised that the world's poor are getting poorer. Up to one third of all children die from malnutrition related diseases before the age of five. In 1977, 750 million people lived in extreme poverty on less than forty pounds per year. One third of the world consumes two thirds of the world's resources.

The Brandt Commission suggested new aid schemes. The emphasis was not charity but enlightened self-interest. Real development in the south would help the north find new markets. But the leaders of the biggest economies dumped the proposals.

There is now in the rich one third a gospel of success. God blesses you with material wealth if you bless him. Try telling that to Christians in most of the world. And do remember, it is now reckoned that most Christians are in the two thirds world, and it is there that churches are growing fastest.

There is no easy answer to these terrible problems. But materialism is the source. There is more than enough food in the world. Most of it is eaten in countries where diet books are best sellers.

3 Materialism ignores ecology

The whole world is God's gift and man's responsibility. We

are burning up the world's non-renewable resources for a frivolous lifestyle. Rain forests, mineral deposits and wildlife are all in devastating decline. These resources are created by God for the benefit of all. Materialism treats them like an unlimited overdraft. But credit is running out.

4 Materialism sets narrow horizons
Advertising tells us possessions matter . . . and nothing else. Value and fulfilment are measured in possessions. Materialism produces a desperately cramped and de-humanised view of people. Bertrand Russell said, "It is preoccupation with possessions more than anything else, that prevents men from living freely and nobly."

5 Materialism feeds on dissatisfaction and worry
You have to be dissatisfied today, so that you spend even more tomorrow. We always feel we need something more. We are driven by an ever restless acquisitiveness. Magpies have nothing on dedicated materialists.

I saw a gardening programme last summer which gave some surprising advice. After all the horticultural tips, the expert added, "Don't forget to stop and enjoy your garden." We're so busy getting more, we're forgetting to enjoy what we've got.

The trouble is, we are all caught in the web of materialism. More than two and a half billion people in the world have never heard the gospel. Up to one billion are starving or malnourished. The "Christian countries" of Europe are full of people who don't know how to receive Christ as Lord and Saviour. Materialism draws at our time, our energy and our values. It wants to leave us no priority in our lives for God.

That's why we must match up our own values against the teaching of Jesus. That's why we must be on guard against easy evasion of Luke's vision of the Church. Materialism cannot cope with "No one claimed that any of his possessions was his own" (Acts 4:32). Materialism has to wriggle away from "there were no needy persons among them" (Acts 4:34).

If we are to rediscover the new community of the Spirit, our materialism must be nailed and nailed again to Christ's cross. The Spirit set the first Christians free. He can deliver us too.

Treasure from heaven

The Spirit united the first Church in a common need and a common experience. All needed Christ for salvation. All were in Christ and had received the same Spirit.

This didn't mean everything was left to instinct. The apostles had to learn to hear the voice of the Spirit through the complaints of new Christians. The Greek Jews began to be neglected in the daily distribution of food (Acts 6:1–6). Spontaneous giving by itself proved inefficient.

Seven men were appointed to look after the needy. But they didn't accept any willing volunteer with suitable practical experience. Those chosen by the Church needed to be "full of the Spirit and wisdom".

Support for each other stretched beyond the local fellowship. When Agabus arrived in Antioch from Jerusalem, the church didn't receive an eye-witness report of an immediate need. He was a prophet and predicted a severe famine throughout the Roman world. Luke stresses this wasn't a lucky guess or natural intuition. Just as the Spirit could speak through preaching and through complaints, Agabus' prophecy came "through the Spirit" (Acts 11:18).

The point of the story isn't that the famine happened, though it did. What matters most is the Antioch Christians' immediate generosity. They accepted the prophecy and acted fast.

Once more they weren't into compulsory communism, but spontaneous self-sacrifice. Each gave willingly "according to his ability". Once more they wanted none in the family left needy. Even before the famine arrived they provided aid. Filled with the same Spirit, they recognised the Judean Christians were their brothers.

The Spirit never calls us only to help other Christians, but that's where self-sacrifice begins. Being God's family is more than words and talk. It costs.

The Spirit turned the first Christians upside down. Ordinary people living ordinary lives were transformed on the inside. It wasn't their natural goodness or friendliness that made non-Christians say in astonishment, "See how these Christians love one another!" It was the power of the Spirit.

We may sum up the Spirit's new community in three contrasts:

From loneliness to new belonging
The Spirit comes to us as individuals. But he is God's *NO* to "I need no one else" individualism. He takes us from wretched isolation to God's new family.

This is a glorious promise for our age of lonely people. We can all belong at last. But there can be no place for snobbery or racial prejudice. The Spirit makes us a family, not a club.

From safety first living to treasure in heaven
When you live for yourself, you have to protect yourself. When this life is all you've got, you don't take risks. The Spirit gives a new family, provides a foretaste of the riches of heaven, and confirms that Jesus is coming again.

In the first church there was no need for insurance (if anyone had wanted to insure such bad risks) because no one would be left in need. Risky living doesn't come easily, but the first Christians followed where the Spirit led.

The Spirit wants to deliver us from safety first living. I don't mean from paying insurance premiums, but from a whole attitude to daily life. It happened for the early Church, so it can happen to us. Not simply as individuals, but together in the community of love.

*From "me-first" materialism to "considered
nothing their own"*

Helping the needy wasn't charity. The one Spirit brought about the one new family, and he was also the one Lord over money and possessions. The pagans couldn't understand this love. Its evangelistic impact was enormous.

This love lasted. In the fourth century, the Emperor Julian received an official report on the Christians' life together "the impious Galileans support not merely their own poor but ours as well."

I am by nature very possessive. It's probably something to do with being the oldest of five children. If I lend something as small as a book, I catch myself thinking, "I hope *my* book comes back in one piece." The Spirit offers to free us from selfishness into willing generosity.

I changed my job two years ago, and we had to hand in our cherished Ford Escort – it was a company car. Now some friends lend us their second car each weekend. It's almost new, and if we damaged it badly, we couldn't afford to repair it. That's risky living in the Spirit of love!

What may the Spirit be saying about the less well off in your fellowship? And what about Western responsibility towards today's majority of Christians in the two thirds world? Can we become again the community of new belonging? By the Holy Spirit it is still possible.

5

NEW CONFIDENCE

When the family moved to Sevenoaks, my life was soon in a spin. I was an average sixteen year old, eager to live in capital letters and to be successful at everything. I had never been religious, never been turned on by choirs and candles, but I was certainly interested in Jesus. New friends soon dragged me to "Contact", a lively Christian youth group.

"Contact" proved irresistible. Teenagers talked about Jesus as a personal friend and Saviour. Their prayers were real and you could see the results. Conversation flowed freely into the small hours about typical mid-teenage concerns – the meaning of life, redistribution of wealth, and who was going out with whom. What's more the girls were pretty!

By early summer I was in a jam. It wasn't girlfriend trouble, and it wasn't an O-level revision crisis. It was Jesus.

Most Saturday nights "Contact" went en masse to Hildenborough Hall, a first-rate Christian conference centre. Through films, rock groups and celebrity interviews, the gospel was presented. Hildenborough was in tune with our needs, always imaginative and relevant. There was never any emotional pressure, but if anyone wanted to respond to Christ, they were invited to echo silently a prayer at the end of the meeting.

That was my problem. Each week the truth of the gospel became more real. I had made some kind of commitment the previous summer, but everything had remained fairly vague and theoretical. I didn't tell anyone, but each week as they prayed on the platform, I knew afresh my need of

Christ. No one else offered promises like his. No one else could take his place. Week after week I echoed that prayer. I wanted to be born again, but how could I be sure? I needed to discover new confidence in Christ's Spirit.

Certain of Christ

Some people hate all certainty. They say being a Christian means being good enough and being religious enough to pass God's entrance exam for heaven. They say that you may hope you are a Christian, but you cannot presume more than that.

The apostle Paul once hoped he pleased Yahweh. He had the finest religious pedigree (Phil 3:4–6) – born into a good family, circumcised at the right time, a scrupulous Pharisee for every detail of the law, and a zealous persecutor of the Christians. But none of this gave him peace with God.

When he met the risen Christ on the road to Damascus, his life was transformed. Compared with Christ's free forgiveness, his religious pedigree was worth nothing. Because he turned to Christ, he lost all his old social prestige.

A religious pedigree couldn't make Paul confident of God's favour. But in Christ, Paul received the "righteousness that comes from God and is by faith". He could never be certain of salvation if it depended on his own goodness. But now he was certain enough to turn from chief persecutor into tireless missionary. Now he was confident, not through pride, but through God's free gift of Christ.

Paul has a reputation for being a difficult writer, but he expresses the heart of the gospel with unforgettable simplicity: ". . . if you confess with your mouth 'Jesus is Lord', and believe in your heart that God raised him from the dead you will be saved. For it is with your heart that you believe and are justified, and it is with your mouth that you confess you are saved" (Rom 10:9–10).

Luther faced the same problem as Paul. He joined a strict

order of monks and kept the rules diligently. He did all in his power to put himself right with God. He was desperate for certain forgiveness and drove himself mercilessly in "fasting, prayer, reading and other good works". Later he reckoned he would soon have destroyed his health, had he kept it up much longer.

Luther understood clearly that all are guilty before God: "However irreproachable my life as a monk, I felt myself in the presence of God to be a sinner with a most unquiet conscience, nor could I believe him to be appeased by the satisfaction I could offer."

When he realised God's standards, lack of certainty over salvation proved a nightmare: "There can be no flight, nor consolation either from within or from without, but all is accusation."

As Luther studied the New Testament he found the new certainty he so desperately needed. Justification is not by human works. No one can ever make up for their past or fully change themselves for the future. Rather, justification is by faith. Christ offers certain salvation: crucified for our sake and risen to bring us new birth.

Now Luther had a new confidence which his years of determined effort couldn't bring. Now his certainty wasn't rooted in his own achievements, but in Christ. His rediscovery of the risen Saviour sparkles with joy – "At this I felt myself straightway born afresh and to have entered through the open gates into paradise itself."

The New Testament promise is clear and consistent. In John's words: "God has given us eternal life, and this life is in his Son. He who has the Son has life" (1 John: 5:11–12). And in Paul's words: "if anyone is in Christ he is a new creation" (2 Cor 5:17). "For it is by grace you have been saved, through faith – and this is not from yourselves, it is the gift of God – not by works, so that no one can boast" (Eph 2:8–9).

The New Testament doesn't leave you on a treadmill of uncertainty. You don't have to keep trying to prove you are good enough for God. The true certainty of the Gospel is centred on Christ alone. This isn't misplaced pride or presumption. When you receive Christ, you receive the love that won't ever let you down: ". . . we have been made holy through the sacrifice of the body of Jesus Christ once for all . . ." (Heb 10:10).

Beginning in the Spirit

The New Testament writers are confident that Christ has died once for all. But a bridge still has to be built from a doctrine on paper to a belief in the heart. Christ died for sinners needs to become Christ died for *me*. Jesus must be seen not merely as a distant controller of the cosmos, but as Lord of *my* life. This turns biblical ideas into saving faith. Head theory becomes heart commitment. That's where the Spirit is crucial.

We have seen Paul's clear summary of conversion: confess with your lips and believe in your heart that Jesus is Lord. Paul goes on to reveal that "Jesus is Lord" is the theme of the true prophet. "Jesus is Lord" is also the focus of true worship in the Spirit.

Only through Jesus can anyone be saved. Only by the Spirit can anyone claim Jesus as Saviour. In fact Jesus explains he begins work even earlier, for the Spirit "convicts the world" of sin (John 16:8). Without the Spirit, none of us could be converted.

This is why Paul was so blunt to the Ephesian followers of John the Baptist. This is why he is so direct in his letter to the Romans: "If anyone does not have the Spirit of Christ, he does not belong to Christ" (Rom 8:9).

Paul doesn't say this to provoke agonised soul-searching among the Roman converts as to whether they have the Spirit. He simply will not allow a rigid line to be drawn between receiving Christ and receiving the Spirit. It is by the "Spirit of Christ" that Christ is received.

Paul has no time for the suggestion that receiving the Spirit is a separate and later experience, to upgrade the believer beyond new life in Christ. Only in the Spirit is that new life possible. Where there is a living confession of Christ as Lord, there is the Spirit.

We have to be equally careful of the opposite overstatement. Paul doesn't say, "I received the Spirit at conversion, so I don't want to talk about him any more." He nowhere suggests that conversion is the sum and the end of the Spirit's activity in the believer. But conversion is quite unmistakably where life in the Spirit begins.

Paul's understanding of the Spirit is penetrating and profound. None of it was written just for academics to theorise over. The Spirit himself breathes through the words of the Bible with unfailing relevance. All Paul's teaching on the Spirit is invaluable and practical for every believer and every fellowship.

For Paul, the Spirit gives new confidence. This is found in assurance of salvation and in the possibility of inner change. He also brings new harmony. This is offered for inner wholeness and also for the unity of the new body of believers, especially through the spiritual gifts. At every stage the Spirit's impact is centred on Christ, because the Spirit always glorifies Jesus and makes us responsive to him. We turn first to new assurance.

Spirit of assurance

The most important passage Paul wrote on assurance is Romans 8:9–27. In a few lines he raises many key ways in which the Spirit provides new confidence. These are not meant for information alone. The Spirit wants to write them on each believer's heart.

1 Christ died for me

"If Christ is in you . . . your spirit is alive" (Rom 8:10). As we have seen, the Spirit makes Christ's death personal to each Christian. He makes the Bible come alive. His presence confirms that when Christ died, *my* salvation was won. The objective cross in past history is the unshakable foundation to my present confidence before God. The Spirit bridges the gap.

2 God with us

"His Spirit lives in you" (Rom 8:11). Jesus was called Immanuel, which means God with us. God was breaking into human history in a new way. Our salvation is complete already, in Christ's cross and resurrection. But that doesn't mean God then removed himself to be distant from mankind. Our relationship is through Christ crucified with Christ risen and glorified.

The Spirit is personal and he is God. He preserves us from dead formalism and religious routine. He makes Christianity come alive. In his Spirit, Jesus is still Immanuel. God is still with us.

3 The prayer of Jesus

"By the Spirit we cry, Abba, father" (Rom 8:15). No Jew had ever dared call God "dear father". They must have been horrified by Jesus. Yahweh was so holy, so awesome, that his name could not even be written down or spoken by many orthodox believers.

Jesus breaks with all traditional reverence by calling God "Abba". Said frivolously it would be close to blasphemy. What Jesus reveals is a unique confidence in God's love, and a unique closeness to him as father.

This prayer had an enormous impact on the first Christians. It is quoted twice by Paul in the original Aramaic, when writing to Greek-speaking Christians (Rom 8:15; Gal 4:6). It seems clear that the actual word of Jesus was used both in public and private prayer – "the Spirit who *calls out*, 'Abba, Father'." (Gal 4:6). The word for a new kind of prayer crossed language barriers along with the gospel.

Only Jesus could call God "Abba" by right. Because Jesus identified with human sin, the new Christians could dare to enter into Jesus' intimate relationship with God. In the one Spirit, all could pray the prayer of the Son.

We have lost the shock of calling God "Abba", and with

it the meaning. In prayer, habit can stifle intimacy. It is possible to pray to God as "Father", and yet relate to him in very formal and distant terms.

The Spirit wants to shock us back into Jesus' closeness to God. This doesn't mean we model our relationship with God on our relationship with our earthly father. It is Jesus who shows us what God the Father is like, and how to relate to him.

The Spirit of Jesus didn't come just to enhance prayer. He came to transform it. God isn't simply with us, nor simply our Saviour, wonderful as those truths about him are. He is Abba, our "dear father", and even our "heavenly dad".

4 Spirit of adoption

"Those who are led by the Spirit of God are sons of God" (Rom 8:14). Some speak as if all people are God's children by birthright. In the New Testament God has only one Son. Without Christ, humans are "slaves to fear", because we have no confidence before God. Our own conscience condemns us.

The Spirit is the Spirit of "adoption" and of "sonship". Adoption under Roman law brought equal rights with natural children. Our status is unreservedly as children of God. Sonship means equality with Christ. With him we become co-heirs.

Of course, this doesn't mean the promise applies only to men. Nor that men are in any sense superior in Christ. Nor that women who are Christians undergo some kind of sex-change after death! What Paul stresses in the shorthand of his age is that all believers are equal, all are adopted, and all are co-heirs with Christ. Once we recognise the full equality of the sexes, we can then translate Paul's meaning as the Spirit of adoption for daughters and for sons alike.

Where the Spirit is, there is adoption. We don't just call God "Abba". We receive the privileges and responsibilities of becoming his children.

In Christ God was reconciling the world to himself. In Christians that ministry of reconciliation must be continued (2 Cor 5:18). To be co-heirs with Christ means that we will share in the unsearchable riches of Christ's glory. But it also means we may share in his sufferings, rejected like him (Phil 1:29).

5 Spirit of inner testimony

"The Spirit testifies with our spirit that we are God's children" (Rom 8:16). For many Christians God remains a celestial policeman. Guilt is the dominant mark of the relationship. He seems to tower over you, ready to clap you in irons at every mistake. Failure and apology dog your tracks. In prayer you begin to feel like the naughty child who can't look his parents straight in the eye.

To be sure, the Spirit convicts us of sin. But he also assures us of forgiveness. Satan however condemns. He accuses as an end in itself. He seeks to crush Christians with a sense of guilt and failure. He is heard in cries of self-rejection – "I'm useless." "There's no way out." "I despair of myself." His accusations are essentially and deliberately destructive.

Conviction by the Spirit is essentially and deliberately positive. The Spirit points out our sin in order to floodlight Jesus as Saviour. He convicts us for forgiveness and for deliverance. Spirit-inspired confession is filled with love and hope.

Wesley wrote of boldly approaching the eternal throne. Guilt is replaced by confidence in Christ. That vibrant assurance can be granted by the Spirit.

Even in our doubts, the Spirit still points to Jesus. He speaks in quiet and sensitive ways when we feel inadequate or undeserving of God's love. Should the pressures of modern life stretch us to breaking point, and should our minds whirl with the demands of work or family, with problem relationships or unpaid bills, Paul promises the Spirit will be with us, assuring us of God's love.

Through inner silence the still small voice of calm will

speak. He whispers in our hearts that we are truly children of God. This too is new confidence from the Spirit.

God knows that we need this inner testimony. But it is elusive when our lives are always too busy and when we live in a turmoil of noise. Music, children, TV and machinery surround us with sound. Anxiety or ceaseless brainstorming buzzes within. I once knew someone whose eyes glazed over after ten minutes of any conversation. It wasn't that he was asleep: he simply couldn't keep his mind off his work for longer than that.

We need to learn again to hear the Spirit's voice on the inside, speaking to our hearts the promises of Scripture. The Spirit's presence is not always measured in decibels or excitement. He tells us we are God's adopted children in countless different but always appropriate ways. We need to help each other to listen.

6 Teaches how to pray

". . . the Spirit helps in our weakness. We do not know what we ought to pray" (Rom 8:26). For a while young children can become devoted to one phrase — "Mommy I want it! Daddy I want it!" But a relationship is more than requests. Even so, prayer is more than petitions. The Lord's prayer is half said before the first thing is asked for.

The closest relationship knows moments when silence is more eloquent than many words. As well as the praise of every trumpet, organ and guitar, our Father invites such silence.

Paul reveals a further kind of prayer. The Spirit prays for Christians (Rom 8:27) just as Christ prays for us in heaven (Rom 8:34). Such is perfect prayer, in total accordance with the Father's will. The same Spirit prays within us (Rom 8:26). What's more, he aligns our prayers with his own prayer and the prayer of Christ.

Words are stretched to the limit in Paul's most daring description of Spirit-led prayer: "the Spirit himself intercedes for us with groans that words cannot express" (Rom 8:26). The Spirit draws us into communion with the inner harmony of the Trinity. In the Spirit, our prayer enters into something of the perfect will and perfect love of God.

7 Power to raise

"He who raised Christ from the dead will also give life to your mortal bodies through his Spirit" (Rom 8:11).

We have seen how the Spirit writes on each converted heart, "Christ was crucified for me." The certainty of Christ's past sacrifice gives us present confidence that we are saved.

But Christ didn't stay dead. God's power raised him, and now God's power lives in us. That means the Easter resurrection wasn't a once-off. We don't have fingers crossed in the vague hope of some kind of survival after death.

The Spirit's power in our lives today provides faith for the future. His presence confirms that just as Jesus was raised, we will be raised. He provides lasting confidence that we are heading for heaven.

8 Promise to raise

"We . . . have the firstfruits of the Spirit" (Rom 8:23).

The power of God means we can be raised. The promise of God is that he will do it.

When the first fruit appears in my garden, the harvest is not far behind. I'm always eager to taste the first fruit. Its quality gives a foretaste of the coming harvest.

The glorious riches of the Spirit are God's first fruit for his children. Our boldest dreams cannot imagine the lavish and inexhaustible riches of the harvest in heaven. God's love is extravagant beyond human measure. In the words of the song, we "ain't seen nothin' yet!"

Paul talks about the Spirit's promise of resurrection in two more ways, as a seal and as a deposit. A merchant used to stamp his seal on goods he had bought, and would come to claim them later. "God . . . set his seal of ownership on us" (2 Cor 1:22). "You were marked in him with a seal, the promised Holy Spirit" (Eph 1:13).

The Spirit is the stamp of God's ownership in the present,

assuring us, claiming new lordship, and setting us apart. At the same time his presence declares that God is coming to claim his own. He is the seal of promise because he fulfils Old Testament prophecy, but also because he promises that Christ will come again.

The Spirit is also a "deposit, guaranteeing what is to come" (2 Cor 1:22, 5:5). He is God's downpayment, "guaranteeing our inheritance until the redemption of those who are God's possession" (Eph 1:14). Our present experience confirms that heaven is ahead. We have the downpayment, and he guarantees that far more will follow.

In modern Greek, the word for "deposit" is used for an engagement ring. The Spirit is the engagement ring for the Church, the Bride of Christ.

9 Yearning for fulfilment

"We . . . groan inwardly as we wait eagerly for our adoption as sons, the redemption of our bodies" (Rom 8:23). To desire something more from life is natural and healthy. It can degenerate into materialism, or it can be enlisted for valuable progress. J. S. Mill said, "Rather a dissatisfied man than a satisfied pig."

For the Christian, a new era has dawned, but present experience is in the overlap. Life has been set on a new footing. The final transformation is certain and will be greater still. The taste we have now prepares us for all that is "not yet".

We already have the Spirit of adoption, yet the final separation from sin and decay is yet to come. Salvation has three tenses. Our salvation *was* completed at the cross. We *are* saved on confession of faith. But not till beyond death or the return of Jesus Christ *will* our salvation be fulfilled.

The Spirit is given for this life. He is concerned with everyday living, not religious escapism. He never makes us superspiritual: too heavenly minded to be any earthly use. But the Spirit does make us yearn for the coming fulfilment. He makes us hungry for heaven.

Confident in the Spirit

Paul gets thoroughly excited about the Spirit. He breathes new confidence into believers in so many different ways. No wonder Paul could consider all his achievements worthless compared with the gift of Christ.

There is one vital fact we must emphasise in conclusion. The Spirit isn't a theory on paper or an impersonal power. *We know him in experience.*

Most of us are very cautious about this. More than thirty years ago Lesslie Newbigin warned: "Theologians today are afraid of the word 'experience' . . . the New Testament writers are free from this fear. They regard the gift of the Holy Spirit as an event which can be unmistakably recognised" (*Household of God*, London 1955).

The Galatian Church began to think of salvation as a reward, merited if you did enough good. To Paul this was disastrous. The Spirit is the Spirit of grace. He is given through Christ. If the Galatians went back to legalism, they would turn their backs on Christ, and forfeit his Spirit. Paul clinches his argument with a question about experience: "I would like to learn just one thing from you: Did you receive the Spirit by observing the law or by believing what you heard?" (Gal 3:2).

Paul doesn't begin his argument with experience. To begin there would risk either redefining Christ every time a new experience appeared, or making a particular experience mandatory for all. Instead Paul begins with Christ. As Tom Smail wrote, "Experience is to be explained in terms of Christ, not Christ in terms of experience" (*Reflected Glory*, London 1975).

We need to seek God, not experience of God. The Spirit draws attention to Christ, not himself. "I looked to the Son of God and the dove of peace flew into my heart. I looked to the dove of peace, but he had flown." Experience is not the Christian's first priority, but that cannot take away the confidence with which Paul questions the Galatians. He is quite certain that the Spirit will have made his presence felt.

Some Christians want to explain it all away – "Must have been caused by strong coffee or all those modern songs!" So often experience of the Spirit is stifled as if all experience is at best dangerous and at worst deranged.

No one suggests that in marriage the only alternative to an engagement contract – clinically negotiating every practical and financial detail before the "troth is plighted" – is impulsive and irresponsible infatuation – loving one today and another tomorrow. Nor should we paint such false opposites about the Spirit.

Paul was confident the Spirit made his presence felt. His arrival was unmistakable. If we are to be truly evangelical, we must rediscover the first Christians' openness to God. If we desire their unrestrained confidence in Christ, we need to receive it through the Spirit, illumining Scripture and kindling in our hearts a living flame of love.

Paul expected a confident answer from every Christian to the question: "Have you received the Spirit?" He expected it not from pure theory, but from living experience.

The Spirit hasn't changed. He can be experienced in the same ways today. He can still provide all the assurance that made Paul so excited. We need to learn again how to be always receptive, always open to his presence.

6

NEW HOLINESS

Some children make enthusiastic gardeners. We heard recently of a two year old helping his Dad. The father had sown seed to the end of a back-breaking row and at last he eased himself upright. His son had been very quiet, and he had been too busy and too stiff to keep looking up. Now at last he could give his full attention. Smiling proudly, the little boy held up a grubby hand. He wanted to give back to Daddy the seeds he had "dropped".

A few years later he'll be sowing his own seed. After an hour or two he'll check whether they have sprouted. Within a week he'll dig some up, to "see how they are getting on".

A good gardener needs patience, and not just with children and other horticultural pests. It's no good sowing, pruning or picking early. There's a right time to plant, and a right time to admire and eat. An immature fruit is no good to anyone if its lifeline to the tree is broken. Lift a plant too early and you may do irreparable damage.

Never neglect a garden. One year I forgot to replenish the slug bait. In the few days before I remembered, the gluttons dined sumptuously on every tender leaf they could find. If Bromley Garden Show included a slug class, my fat and greedy specimens would have won first prize. A gardener's patience needs to be watchful: nothing can be taken for granted except the arrival of more greenfly.

The Spirit brings new responsibilities as well as new privileges. The sons and daughters of God are also his new servants. Called to be in Christ, we are also called to be like him. Adoption is secure in what Christ has already done. Holiness is a gradual heart change.

When Luther tried to save himself, he didn't only realise he was guilty before God. He also discovered his own "impotence for good" and came to "despair of his own strength". In the same way Jeremiah saw that we cannot change ourselves. Just as the leopard cannot change his spots, we all seem preprogrammed for sin. Jeremiah's conscience told him there must be a better way. His prophecy confirmed that there was: "I will put my law in their minds and write it on their hearts" (Jer 31:33).

We have seen that the Spirit of Christ gives new confidence of salvation. We can be confident of freedom from the guilt of our past. We can be confident of freedom in the coming resurrection from the last clinging stains of our old life. He also gives confidence for inner deliverance from the tyranny of ingrained sin.

Without the Spirit there can be no fruit of the Spirit. With the Spirit, the fruit is the spontaneous demonstration of his presence. The Spirit bears fruit just as sap in the spring pushes out new buds.

Fruit usually matures gradually. When Paul writes of fruit it immediately suggests organic growth, not instant moral transformation. "Character is the produce of a lifetime" (John Stott *Baptism and Fullness* Leicester 1975).

Our local nursery had a display last autumn of newly developed bulbs for the gardener in a hurry. The foliage was perfect. Flowering was instantaneous. Genetic engineering has been making great strides, but I didn't expect anything like this. They were ideal for the instant garden . . . so long as you like plastic.

There are no instant answers for inner transformation in this life. A plastic veneer of superficial piety is no fruit of the Spirit. The Spirit cultivates a garden which has your lifetime to mature.

The real test of inner change is not on a Sunday. Religious behaviour is often put on with smart shoes or a tie. If someone stands on your toe are they a clumsy oaf? Never, at least out loud, at the morning service! The critical moment is midweek. You're tired, no other

Christians are in sight, and then someone stands on your toe. Are they *now* a clumsy oaf?

Inner change is tested in your off-guard reaction. It may be an eruption that makes Vesuvius look like a failed firework. It may be in that split second before you regain your composure. Instinctive reactions reveal the state of our heart.

In our deepest instincts the Spirit wants to make us more like Jesus. He's an open heart not a plastic surgeon. There may be setbacks and many operations. Progress won't always be apparent. But left alone, we couldn't begin to heal ourselves. We must allow his skilful work time.

Paul explains the Spirit's target of holiness and assures us the Spirit is at work on the inside. He is very frank about the Christian's experience of inner struggle. But he never allows us to lose sight of the hope of inner renewal. Paul will be our chief guide to confidence in the Spirit for new holiness now.

The target of holiness

If you want to hit a target, you need to know what to avoid. The Galatian Christians were free in Christ, but Paul warned them not to "gratify the desires of the sinful nature" (Gal 5:16). Part of each Christian wants nothing better than self-indulgence. But the Spirit of holiness calls us to "serve one another in love" (Gal 5:13).

Paul records the "acts of the sinful nature" (Gal 5:19 –21). They read like the stocklist of a vast hypermarket of sin. There's something here for every kind of self-indulgence. They catalogue the tawdry world behind the headlines of the gossip press: sexual immorality and de- bauchery, witchcraft and orgies, selfish ambition and fits of rage. Most of us will never live our way through all the listed vices. But together they sum up what's wrong with our species.

The trouble with Paul is the same as the trouble with Jesus: both will have no compromise with sin. Tucked in with the excesses most of us avoid, there are many "respectable" vices. Party spirit (exclusive in-crowds) and arguments are found in the best of circles. A little envy and jealousy are surely standard fitments, not optional extras for society's outcasts?

Paul doesn't mix them in to play down the worst faults. He does it to show that all sin has the same source. We cannot allow any "work of the sinful nature" to become acceptable through familiarity or regular use. According to the New Testament, all are deadly. Jeremy Taylor concluded, "No sin is small. No grain of sand is small in the mechanism of a watch."

Sin is easy to spot in others. Psychologists tell us we often condemn most strongly in others the things we like least in ourselves. The Spirit holds up the mirror of conviction, and he shows us the sin that's our own.

Paul turns from the darker side of self to consider "whatsoever is lovely". The fruit of right living doesn't come from what is sometimes called our "better nature". Good fruit comes from God's Spirit. ". . . the fruit of the Spirit is love, joy, peace, patience, kindness, goodness, faithfulness, gentleness and self-control. Against such things there is no law" (Gal 5:22–3).

The Spirit produces fruit, not a mixture of fruits. It is singular, not plural. This needs to be emphasised time and again. You may be more keen on joy than self-control, more keen on goodness than gentleness. But that's not the way of the Spirit. If you find traces of one or two in your life, you can't settle back in complacency. This isn't a list from which to pick and choose.

The characteristics of the one fruit are like an apple's stalk and pips and flesh and skin. If any is missing, the fruit is incomplete and deformed. The target of the Spirit is to produce all these characteristics in every Christian.

Countless books have been written which work methodically through Paul's list. We don't have space for that. But we need at least to notice these five points:

* It is difficult to analyse any one of these qualities in complete isolation from the rest. In practice they overlap. This underlines their indivisible unity as one fruit.
* The fruit represents a new way of relating to God, to others and to ourselves. For example, we are made at peace with God by Christ, which promises a new inner peace, and this permits at least the possibility of radiating a new peace to others. You only have to be with some people a few minutes for the peace in their heart to begin to warm your own.
* The fruit is designed for everyday living. These aren't specialised qualities for clergy or missionaries. The Spirit is practical. His fruit in all Christians is potentially of the same kind.
* The fruit is immediately recognisable. You can't miss these qualities in someone. What's more, they are immediately attractive. These are the ideals behind countless new year resolutions. If you were asked what qualities are most desirable in life, this list sums them up.
* This fruit is beyond any law. No one can make kindness or goodness illegal. No law can make joy or patience compulsory. These are inner qualities which radiate in a new way of living. They cannot thrive as external additions to an unchanged life. Good works are the result of salvation, not how to achieve it.

Every owner of an apple tree longs for its boughs to be heavy with fruit, like the master-growers' orchards in the Garden of England. All but the most degenerate people yearn for a bumper crop of the qualities Paul lists. But only by the Spirit can we bear God's fruit. "It's no good tying apples on to a dead tree" (Michael Green, *New Life, New Lifestyle*, London 1973).

The promise of holiness

Love isn't by accident the first in Paul's list. Love is the sum of these qualities and the heart of the fruit. Love is the white light which enters a prism: the other virtues are a rainbow and together they make up love.

These glorious virtues form an identikit picture of the fruit of the Spirit. Suppose that Christianity was illegal, and this identikit picture was issued to make arrests. We have to ask a painful question: would there be enough likeness for me to be convicted?

One life showed these qualities in perfect harmony. One life could be summed up by love. That, of course, was the life of Jesus.

Jesus was immediately striking and wholly admirable. His love saw behind the public face of others to their hidden needs. Rice and Lloyd-Webber's Superstar cried to the crowds, "Heal yourselves!" But the real Jesus kept on loving, kept on healing, though his body ached with exhaustion.

When none of his disciples was prepared to wash the feet of the rest, Jesus the Master became the servant of them all. When, on trumped up charges, he endured the bone-wrenching agony of the cross, his prayer wasn't one of self-vindication – "Show them I'm your Son!" Instead, other people stayed his top priority – "Father, forgive them, for they don't know what they are doing."

Jesus loved not just the lovable, but everyone. He loved not for what he could gain out of it, but because he saw each man and woman through the eyes of God. Their needs came before his own well-being.

Jesus said a man's greatest love was to lay down his life for his friends. But God's gift-love went further. Jesus' self-sacrifice was made "while we were yet sinners".

Bernard of Clairvaux was given rare and eloquent insight into the love of God: "I know that I must love him more than I love myself, because, beside myself, he gives me also himself, a gift of infinitely greater worth . . . God deserves exceeding love from us, a love that has no measure" (*On the Love of God* Oxford, 1982).

Jesus' way of living couldn't be put on with a Sunday suit. His instincts were as selfless as his actions. His whole being resounded with the harmony of God's love. Holiness means living like Jesus.

God's intention is that Christians "bear the family likeness of his Son" (Rom 8:29 J. B. Phillips). As the fruit of the Spirit forms within, we will indeed become more like Jesus. It doesn't take much self-examination to know this can only come about as a miracle.

Paul longed for the Galatians to stop dabbling in fruitless attempts at spiritual self-improvement. God's plan and Paul's desire were that "Christ is formed in you" (Gal 4:19). By grace we are in Christ. By the Spirit, Christ is formed in us.

Desire for change tends to run far ahead of actual transformation. But it isn't all wishful thinking. Paul explains we can take comfort in wanting to be more holy. This desire isn't an end in itself, but it is a sure sign that God is already at work: "for it is God who works in you to will and to act according to his good purpose" (Phil 2:13).

The Spirit makes us "hunger and thirst for righteousness". He makes Paul's description of the fruit and the character of Christ so attractive. Yearning for change isn't just the first step towards holiness. It's the Spirit's first prompting.

Sin is a smog which conceals our individuality under its grimy film. The Spirit wants to liberate our true individuality from the crushing sameness of sin. The Spirit doesn't turn us into Holy Joes, all religious and out of touch. Jesus wasn't like a clerical character in a TV sitcom. He was more attractively human than anyone else in Galilee. The fruit of the Spirit is the character of Jesus.

God loves the unique *you*. No one else can replace you. The Spirit of holiness desires to set the real you free. The more you become like Jesus, the more free you are to become your real self. Perfect freedom is not "doing your own thing". Perfect freedom is found in serving the God who made us and has delivered us from bondage to sin.

The struggle for holiness

Growing in holiness is like riding a bike. If you stop peddalling, you fall off.

The journey into holiness isn't like five minutes on your bike. It's more like cycling round the world. To get there you need to set an immediate target you can achieve, even if it's only the next lampost. But you shouldn't take your eyes off the final destination. It's no good settling in Manhattan if you are headed for New Delhi.

I remember meeting someone who said they'd stopped sinning. As a new Christian they'd had the usual problems. But now old sins were dead. There were still occasional lapses – they had sinned once about a week before – but for the mature in Christ, the journey was mainly downhill.

I looked in my heart and knew this couldn't be true for me. I looked at God's standards, and saw holiness was an uncompromising mountain range. Sin doesn't simply blemish occasional actions. It stains the very fabric of human life.

Paul's version of mature Christian living is quite different. He hasn't reached destination holiness. Nor is he coasting downhill. In fact he is peddling harder than ever. "Not that I have already obtained all this, or have already been made perfect, but I press on to take hold of that for which Christ Jesus took hold of me" (Phil 3:12).

Paul never loses sight of the Spirit's promised fruit. Christ took hold of him to draw him into holiness. But neither does he forget his own continual failings.

Paul obviously feels this might not register at first. He can hear some Philippians saying, "If anyone has reached perfection, surely it is the apostles?" And so he repeats himself even more vigorously in the next two verses. Paul has *not* arrived, but like a single-minded athlete, he is more determined than ever to "go for it" – "Brothers, I do not consider myself yet to have taken hold of it. But one thing I do: Forgetting what is behind and straining towards what is ahead, I press on towards the goal . . ." (Phil 3:13–14). Just in case anyone now feels superior to Paul, confident that they at least have finished the race, he adds, "All of us who are mature should take such a view of things" (Phil 3:15).

Continuing struggle means continuing weakness. Paul's words in Romans 7:15 inspired the Anglican General Confession – "We have left undone those things which we ought to have done: and we have done those things which we ought not to have done: and there is no health in us."

Augustine knew many inner conflicts before his conversion. But those difficult beginnings had been left far behind when he prayed as a mature Christian – "Heal me, in whose eyes I am now become a problem to myself. That is my infirmity" (*Confessions* X:33 trans E. M. Blaiklock, London 1983).

John Donne considered the cross one Easter, and saw there the fire of God's love. He looked in his own heart and saw flickering embers. In shame he hid his face. He knew that God alone could deal with such deep-rooted weakness.

> O think me worth your anger, punish me,
> Burn off my rusts, and my deformity,
> Restore your Image, so much, by your grace,
> That you may know me, and I'll turn my face.
> (Good Friday, 1613. Riding Westward)

The New Testament promises a continuing struggle with continuing weakness. But we are also promised new confidence.

First, *temptation will not overwhelm us.* God knows how much each individual can take. He won't let his children be crushed. "But when you are tempted, he will also provide a way out so that you can stand up under it" (1 Cor 10:13).

Second, *forgiveness is always available* (1 Jn 2:2). In

102

Christ, there is no condemnation (Rom 8:1). Helder Camara has said, "Being holy means getting up immediately every time you fall, with humility and joy. It doesn't mean never falling into sin. It means being able to say, "Yes, Lord, I have fallen one thousand times. But thanks to you I've got up a one thousand and one times."

Third, *for those who press on the fruit will grow*. We can be controlled by the Spirit, and not our sinful nature (Rom 8:9). Mature Christians don't stop sinning. But they know more and more their own need of holiness. And in the power of the Spirit they continue the struggle. "To obtain the gift of Christian holiness is the work of a lifetime" (Newman).

The journey may not be easy, nor completed in five minutes. But the struggle is worth continuing, for the destination is heaven – "the glorious freedom of the children of God" (Rom 8:21).

John Donne thought he was dying in 1523, and so he wrote a final confession. The sickness left him, but the poem was set to music, and was often sung by the "choristers of St Paul's Cathedral". His prayer for the struggle of holiness is a poem of painful honesty but clearsighted faith. It could be written on the heart of every Christian.

A HYMN TO GOD THE FATHER

Will you forgive that sin where I begun,
    Which is my sin, though it were done before?
Will you forgive those sins through which I run
    And do them still, though still I do deplore?
      When you have done, you have not done,
      for I have more.

Will you forgive that sin, by which I've won
    Others to sin, and made my sin their door?
Will you forgive that sin which I did shun
    A year or two, but wallowed in a score?
      When you have done, you have not done
      for I have more.

I have a sin of fear, that when I've spun
My last thread, I shall perish on the shore;
Swear by yourself that at my death, your Son
Shall shine as he shines now, and shone before;
And having done that, you have done,
I have no more.

The hope of holiness

If you see holiness as an effortless joyride, you'll come down to earth with a bump. The illusion of instant perfection can lead in the end to despair: "Either there's something wrong with me, since I can't change myself, or God has rejected me." When we hide our struggle for holiness behind a slick Sunday smile, those who don't know us may think we find holiness easy. Lack of teaching on the struggle brings a harvest of needless problems. Disillusion is a tough price to pay for misplaced idealism. "Many of the young people I meet are living defeated, disillusioned, and disappointed lives even after coming to Christ . . . because they have had no proper teaching at this precise point . . . the old force is not yet dead or wholly renewed . . . It fights every inch of the way" (Billy Graham, *The Holy Spirit*, London 1979). Anyone who plans to be a saint in a day, risks tomorrow being a hardened sinner. The best fruit can't be forced.

Youth and idealism often go together. But can you teach an old dog new tricks? Where the hope of holiness has never found a home, a life of little sins becomes accepted. Resignation speaks familiar words:

"That's how I am, and there's nothing you can do about it."

"Ours has always been a proud family."

"If there's one thing I can't stand . . ."

No life is barren ground for the fruit of the Spirit. He who had the power to raise Jesus from the dead, has the power to change your life. If God has begun his work in you, don't prevent him continuing it.

Is there someone you just don't get along with? Do they seem always to "rub you up the wrong way"? Don't blame them for it. David Watson used to recommend you turn the blame on yourself. "You shouldn't have a wrong way to rub up!"

An old friend called Mark used to think the fruit of the Spirit simply meant trying your best. God gave new birth, but after that it was all up to you. In the end Mark had to face facts. He couldn't change himself. The joy of the gospel was this: he didn't have to, at least not on his own.

At last Mark could pray in a new way. God doesn't just offer forgiveness for the past, he promises to grow fruit in the present. The change in Mark wasn't total, but it was unmistakable. Now he worked to change himself, not on his own but in the Spirit's power.

Six months later a friend returned from Canada. Her first question to Mark said it all: "What's got into you?"

The struggle of holiness warns that there are moments of sudden reversal. Paul warned that no Christian is above temptation (Gal 6:1). But we need to grasp at the same time the hope of holiness. God doesn't guarantee to work fast, but there are in many lives moments of sudden and dramatic improvement.

Hope of holiness is vital. But by itself it isn't enough. Whether fruit comes fast or slow, we need to see it in practice.

Paul makes it quite clear that salvation is God's work, but it still calls for our cooperation. He tells the Colossians, "you died with Christ" (Col 2:20). Then he adds, "put to death your earthly nature" (Col 3:5). He says the Galatians "have crucified the sinful nature" (Gal 2:20), but also warns them not to sow to it, but to "sow to please the Spirit" (Gal 6:8).

Paul is not playing with words. Our salvation is already complete at Christ's cross. But now we have to claim it, and live in the light of it, first in conversion and then with every effort, day by day.

The pursuit of holiness

Jesus called us to take up our cross daily and follow him (Luke 9:23). The Spirit wants Christians to pursue holiness with every fibre and every sinew of our being.

1 The Spirit requires self-denial

This is not very fashionable. But it needed self-denial for Jesus to go to the cross.

A friend of ours faced strong sexual temptation. Many Christians have struggled with this in the past. Many have shown that it may not be easy, but it remains possible to deny lust and keep in step with the Spirit. This is particularly possible where there is a caring local fellowship.

Ours is the instant generation: "Without sex, no fulfilment. And why wait for fulfilment?" The promise is popular, but empty and deceitful. Sadly, self-denial seemed too much for our friend. He chose sex, not the Spirit.

John Chrysostom was the most popular preacher of the fourth century. He didn't hide the need for self-denial from his congregation. Holiness can be hard work:

> The younger athletes practise on the bodies of their comrades the attack that one day they will have to launch on their opponents. Let this be a challenge to you. Practise yourself in the discipline of true religion. You see many Christians unable to resist the paroxysms of anger, and others set on fire by the flames of lust. Practise resistance against such passions (*Chrysostom and his Message*, from the 33rd homily on Matthew. Trans. by S. Neill, London 1962).

2 The Spirit may require material loss

Some Christians' possessions are all-absorbing. Their lives are so full, there's no room left for holiness. Others are dedicated to a career that demands, quite simply, total commitment. Some live double lives: God at home, Mammon in the office. Before new fruit can be grown successfully, undergrowth and dead wood need to be uprooted. "Some persons, laden with wealth . . . make no progress nor come to harbour, because they have not the courage to break with some whim, attachment or affection . . . Yet all they have to do is to set sail resolutely, cut the ship's cable, or rid themselves of the clinging, sucking-fish of desire" (John of the Cross, *Ascent of Mount Carmel* 1:XI:iv, trans E. Hamilton, London 1976).

3 The Spirit desires continuous growth

Holiness is for ever. The Spirit wants an increasing harvest of holiness, not a bowl of yesterday's fruit.

Some old people's faces are lined with laughter. Every wrinkle seems to smile. To be with them makes you feel closer to God and glad to be alive. Others grow more stubborn and glum every year, till the features grow fixed in a scowl. "Where habits are sown, a character is grown."

When Leonardo da Vinci was painting the Last Supper, he looked for a model for Christ. There is a story that he chose a chorister in one of the churches in Rome. The young man, Pietro Bardinelli, was said to be "lovely in life and features".

Years passed, and the painting was nearly finished. Only one disciple was left to paint, Judas Iscariot. Now Leonardo looked for a model whose face was hardened and distorted by riotous living. He found at last a Roman beggar, with a face so villainous he shuddered at the sight of it.

He hired the man and painted his face. When he was about to pay and dismiss him he commented, "I've not yet found out your name."

"I'm Pietro Bardinelli, who sat as your model for Christ." (adapted from a story in the *Indian Christian*).

We need to examine ourselves. In the time since my conversion, what has life done to my Christ-likeness? Jesus died: is my sinful nature being put to death in him? Jesus rose: does his resurrection shine out through the changes in my life? Jesus reigns: am I confident in Jesus as Lord, not only in how I worship, but in how I live?

There's no substitute for the fruit of the Spirit. Nothing else can make you more like Jesus. No other aim can bring you closer to God.

The Spirit of Christ is the Spirit of holiness. Holy is his name and holiness is his intention in every believer. Give the Spirit time to change you. Give him room. And give him all the energy you have.

7

NEW WHOLENESS

Some Christians aren't very keen on the Spirit. He gets the blame for anything they don't like. One warned me that St Aldate's, Oxford, had gone "extremely charismatic". Intrigued I asked what he meant. "Well," he explained, "they now shake hands in the Communion service!"

I think Michael Green and David Prior might have laughed. I explained that this was a normal liturgical practice with a long history, going back to the greeting of a "holy kiss" in the early Church. It is not by any means a certain mark of "charismania". Christians even shook hands during the peace at Westminster Abbey, in the presence of the Queen, when the Alternative Service Book 1980 was launched.

Some churches now encourage "heavenly hugs" while avoiding "carnal cuddles". Saying the grace with arms linked can be a marvellous expression of love in the united fellowship. But others still consider sinister the briefest touch of hands.

I remember my first European publishers' convention. You only shake an English businessman's hand once. That is the limit of normal physical contact. But Europeans shake hands time and again. A handshake when first introduced. A handshake when the meeting is over. If they see you again, a handshake again. They even shake hands with their friends and colleagues.

For the more reserved subjects of Her Majesty Queen Elizabeth, such astonishing physical excess takes some getting used to. You see some almost disguising the existence of their arms to minimise the daily dose of handshakes!

The British are notorious sufferers from the "don't touch me" disease. We live from day to day in physical isolation. After that first handshake, the straightjacket is put back on. If a train arrives at our station with just one compartment empty, we will find it, and that is where we will sit.

The handshake didn't originally express great warmth of feeling. It simply reassured someone that there wasn't a sword in your right hand. The hug and kiss were more suited to family and friends. When even a handshake is suspicious or excessive in worship, we have lost touch not only with each other, but also with our own bodies.

Jesus didn't have the English disease. He knew that lepers were treated not just as outcasts but as untouchables. The warmth of his hand on theirs was a tender expression of God's love, even before he healed them.

The disciples' feet were dirty and sweaty, but when Jesus washed them it was more than an act of hygiene. His touch expressed his selfless and serving love. The disciples knew that God didn't just love mankind: in Jesus, each received God's love individually.

When John asked Jesus who would betray him, they were reclining for a meal. John leant his head back against Jesus' chest (John 13:25). Touch was a normal part of a close and healthy relationship. Touch speaks more tenderly than words.

It's the same with emotions. I remember hearing of a young Christian who suffered terribly when his father died. It wasn't simply the bereavement. His father had told him it would be a "good witness" not to shed a tear. The English stiff upper lip was meant to grow quite rigid after conversion.

All the emotion of loss was bottled up inside. It turned ever more sour until he could contain it no longer. It burst out like steam from a fractured pressure cooker. The poor boy tried to take his life.

Jesus knew his emotions and he wasn't scared of them. He was free to use them, and so, before the grave of his good friend Lazarus he did the natural thing. He wept in public, without disguise and without disgrace.

Jesus was complete. There is a wonderful wholeness about him in the gospels. He gave time to the needy without begrudging it. But he was never a workaholic. Once when he climbed into the disciples' boat he was exhausted. He didn't try to hide it. They were the sailors and he'd been busy all day. So he was quite prepared to take forty winks and let the experts get on with it. Only when the storm grew too fierce for them to handle did he wake up.

Jesus knew himself and he accepted himself. He seemed to have an instinctive grasp of what made each person tick. He knew when to be firm, but was never too firm. He always had the right words for each occasion and for each person.

Jesus was a man supremely at peace with God and himself. Psychologists might call him the "fully integrated personality". We have seen that Jesus revealed God's holiness in action. He also lived out human wholeness.

Will the real me stand up?

Jesus' human wholeness stands a long way from common experience. Our lives seem a box full of jig-saw oddments: we can't make the pieces fit a single pattern.

Sometimes we surprise ourselves. We do or think or say something that seems quite out of character. It's like catching a glimpse of someone in a mirror and looking twice before you realise it's you. Peter Sellers delighted millions with his many characters, but he couldn't always make out which was really himself.

One way out is to build a life which only uses some of the pieces. Jimmy did that. For many years his life had gone from bad to worse. But now Jimmy was as carefree as a teenager. Whether from disease or some strange accident, a mind that couldn't cope had erased itself.

Jimmy's memory was lost forever. He was forty-nine, but the last thirty years might never have happened. If you left the room for two minutes he forgot he had ever met you. His life continually evaporated.

In a New York hospital in 1975 he recalled to his doctor his early years. He could remember as much of his child-hood as anyone. Then something strange happened. His memories didn't just grow more vivid when he told how he joined the Navy near the end of World War Two. He switched to the present tense. His doctor takes up the story:

A sudden, improbable suspicion seized me.

"What year is this, Mr R.?" I asked, concealing my perplexity under a casual manner.

"Forty-five, man. What do you mean?" He went on, "We've won the war, FDR's dead, Truman's at the helm. There are great times ahead."

"And you, Jimmy, how old would you be?"

Oddly, uncertainly, he hesitated a moment, as if engaged in calculation. "Why, I guess I'm 19, Doc. I'll be 20 next birthday."

Looking at the grey-haired man before me, I had an impulse for which I have never forgiven myself – it was, or would have been, the height of cruelty had there been any possibility of Jimmy's remembering it.

"Here," I said, and thrust a mirror toward him. "Look in the mirror and tell me what you see. Is that a 19-year-old looking out from the mirror?"

He suddenly turned ashen and gripped the sides of the chair . . . he whispered [curses] . . . "What's going on? What's happened to me? Is this a nightmare? Am I crazy? Is this a joke?" – and he became frantic, panicky.

"It's okay, Jim," I said soothingly. "It's just a mistake. Nothing to worry about." I took him over to the window . . . He regained his colour and started to smile, and I stole away, taking the hateful mirror with me. (Two minutes later, all was forgotten.) (Oliver Sacks, *Awakenings*, reprinted from the New York Review of Books, in *The Observer*, January 1985.)

When Jimmy looked in the mirror, he couldn't see himself. That sense of not belonging is very common today. Nothing quite seems to fit. It's not that we suffer erased memories, but there is an unbridgeable gap between the way we live and the way we feel life ought to be. We sometimes don't feel at home either in the everyday world, or even on the inside. Pink Floyd sang of someone else in my head apart from me.

This "alienation" is a twentieth century preoccupation. Writers describe alienation from ourselves, our work and each other. Tom Stoppard's *Rosencrantz and Guildenstern are Dead* is an extremely funny parable of modern man's lostness. These two very ordinary people with extra-ordinary names keep bumping into characters from Shakespeare's *Hamlet*, who speak in Elizabethan poetry from the quill of the bard and give orders to our two heroes. They just don't belong in this strange world, but it controls them, and even arranges their deaths. Life doesn't fit, but they are helpless to change it.

Jean Paul Sartre looked at the way people can destroy each other and concluded "Hell is other people." He said that conventional fiction is a reassuring lie, because it provides a beginning, middle and end. Novels tell us life has a shape, order and meaning, which is what we all long for. But real life is a series of chance collisions, an accident without a purpose.

The Old Testament is no stranger to alienation. Genesis 1–11 shows sin to be its source. The first act of disobedience leads quickly to evasion of responsibility. Adam tries to persuade God it was "all her fault".

Man is sentenced to sweat and toil: work becomes an unfortunate and often unenjoyable necessity. A new conflict arises between humans and nature. "Cursed is the ground because of you; through painful toil you will eat of it all the days of your life. It will produce thorns and thistles for you" (Gen 3:17–18). Soon the first murder happens and like most other murders it is within the family. After that there develops an explosive increase of lust, idolatry, pride and irreligion. Sin isn't a one-off. It multiplies faster than rabbits. Paul explores four different kinds of alienation. Together they sum up the dissatisfaction at the heart of life, and man's quest for something more.

1 Cut off from God
Many express an aching need for God that nothing else can satisfy. But actions and attitudes often go against that need. "People are alienated from God, being his enemies in their minds" (Col 1:21). Books that attack Jesus make headlines. Call him a myth or a mushroom, or say a double was crucified while Jesus escaped with Mary Magdalene to France – any nonsense will do – and you have a bestseller.

2 Cut off from nature
The pollution and destruction of natural resources is a terrible legacy of the industrial age. But alienation goes deeper than that. "Nature is subjected to frustration and disorder by man who is alienated from it" (Rom 8:20).

I love fell-walking. Within minutes you can be alone with nature. Around you is spectacular beauty; freshly shooted grass clambers over unconquerable volcanic rock, ages old. Yet even as the glorious beauty quickens your pulse and fills you with delight and praise, you have a feeling that you don't somehow fit.

Wordsworth was never more at home than when alone in the Lake District. His poetry will last for as long as poetry is read. Yet not even Wordsworth ever felt fully at home. We don't quite belong in nature any more.

> Waters on a starry night
> Are beautiful and fair;
> The sunshine is a glorious birth;
> But yet I know, wher'er I go,
> that there hath passed away a glory from the earth.
> (Ode: Intimations of immortality ii)

3 Cut off from each other
You don't need to teach children selfishness, it is there at

birth. "Mine" and "want it" soon turn into shoving other children away from their toys. If war wasn't an automatic repeat in human history, each new generation would have to invent it. But real war never lives up to the movies. An American soldier killed an enemy guerrilla with a knife, but then said, "I felt sorry. I don't know why I felt sorry. John Wayne never felt sorry."

Through race and class and caste, through insult and inability to trust, we cut ourselves off from each other. The "works of the flesh" are a catalogue of mutual hostility and antagonism. But in our heart of hearts we don't want it that way. While the divorce rate rises faster and faster, most people still long for a loving relationship that lasts.

4 Cut off from ourselves

In Romans chapter seven Paul describes inner or self-alienation. Life for Paul is made up of contradictory fragments. We cannot see clearly an overall pattern. Left to ourselves we have no self-assembly chart or suitable glue. God's law shows how life can be lived: loving God with all we've got and loving as ourselves our neighbours throughout the global village. But those who try hardest to fulfil God's commands conclude it is simply not possible without Christ.

The more we look inside the more uncertain we become about ourselves. We once thought madness and sanity to be as different as black and white. Now we are told that sanity is just a darker shade of grey. For John Donne, this inner conflict became almost unbearable, apart from Christ:

O to vex me, contraries meet in one.

Only in Jesus do we see the human wholeness and harmony intended by God. Only through Jesus can that deepest wholeness begin to be recovered. For it was Jesus who promised: "I have come that you might have life, and have it abundantly" (John 10:10).

The heartbeat of wholeness

New leaves each spring always seem a miracle. A few weeks before so many plants seemed dead. Until the earth grows warm again, the plant's life withdraws deep inside. But for new buds to break out, that life must already be within.

It's not much help talking about life's problems if there is no way forward. If we want to recover human wholeness, we have to begin with the love of God.

We need to see ourselves in resurrection light. Sin and death are already defeated. Our lives may be in fragments. But God has already acted. New wholeness can bud because God's love comes first.

John tells us time and again that God is love. We know God's love because he sent Jesus to die for us. We love God because he first loved us. John keeps spelling it out because it takes time to sink in.

Jesus recognised the same problem. He taught very clearly how much God loves us. But his words are so astonishing that we tend to either misread them or play them down – ". . . you have loved them even as you have loved me . . ." (John 17:23) Jesus insists that God really loves us.

As much as we deserve?
                    Far more.
As much as anything he created?
                    Even more.
How much then?
                    As much as he loved Jesus.

If Jesus hadn't taught it, no other Christian would dare to suggest it. Jesus is God's only Son. Jesus shares in the perfect love of the Trinity. Jesus delights in the will of the Father, and never rejected him through sin. *But God loves each one of us as much as he loves Jesus.*

". . . be absolutely certain that our Lord loves you, devotedly, and individually: loves you just as you are. How

often that conviction is lacking even in those souls who are
most devoted to God! They make repeated efforts to love
him, they experience the joy of loving and yet how little
they know, how little they realise, that God loves them
incomparably more than they will ever know how to love
him. Think only of this and say to yourself, 'I am loved by
God more than I can either conceive or understand!' Let
this fill all your soul and all your prayer and never leave
you" (A. de Tourville, *Letters of Spiritual Direction*,
Oxford 1982).

This is the spark of life in the heart of darkness. This is
the certain hope that makes wholeness more than a fanciful
dream. In all our failings, weakness and self-contradiction,
God loves us. He has not only made forgiveness secure. He
makes a new inner harmony possible.

The heartbeat of wholeness is the lifegiving love of God.
Only the Spirit can make this real on the inside. Only by the
Spirit dare we say, "God truly loves me as much as he loves
Jesus!" Only then can the sap of the Spirit begin to flow.
Only then does a new inner harmony begin to bloom.

Five steps to harmony

God loves us just as we are, but he loves us too much to
leave us there. Jesus forgave the woman caught in adultery
but told her to sin no more. Jesus befriended fishermen,
and then invited them to follow him. The Bible reveals five
key steps to prepare for true wholeness.

1 Earthly appetites
Jesus warned that a lustful look is adultery in the heart. It
turns another person into a sex object. Paul said that
gluttony is idolatry. It turns food into a god. Such appetites
can take complete control, so that we become less than
human. To describe human excesses as animal urges seems
unfair to animals!

I remember my one and only motorbike. It wasn't
exactly a mean machine. But for a while it was the pride of

my life. When we prayed in church, I just couldn't get it out of my mind.

A greedy society is driven by earthly appetites. An American specialist who counsels the terminally ill has concluded that the more someone hungers after material things, the harder it is to come to terms with dying. If earthly appetites are all that you have, there is no possible hope beyond the grave.

One way out of the power of these desires is extreme self-denial. Some early Christians took a vow of celibacy within marriage, so as not to be "defiled." Others punish or even mutilate their bodies, to try to ensure full control. These aren't solutions, they are self-rejection.

Uncontrolled appetites are destructive. The Bible makes that quite clear. Lust caused David to murder. The Israelites saw that pride comes before a fall. And Jesus warned that the root of all evil is the love of money.

Earthly appetites have positive value in their right place. The Song of Solomon warns not to awake love before it is ready, but it is also a sensual celebration of the delight of human love. The ancient Hebrews didn't only worship God through singing. They also praised him through special banquets. So while gluttony creates a false idol, God delights in true pleasure in food, just as he gave men and women the gifts of love and sex.

The New Testament ideal is neither to be overwhelmed by earthly appetites, nor to reject them altogether. The Spirit is able to bring them under control. He can also bring them into harmony.

2 The distorted self

A dedicated businessman may sacrifice his family to his ambition. He sees his true value only in career and salary. A film star may be spoilt and lonely. But fame paints her glossy image as perfect as can be. False values distort a person. A part is made into the whole.

When Socrates was about to die, he wanted his sons to be freed from the stupidity of self-distortion — "Punish my sons, gentlemen, when they grow up; give them this same pain I gave you if you think they care for money or anything else better than virtue; and if they have the reputation of being something when they are nothing, reproach them, as I reproach you, that they do not take care for what they should, and think they are something when they are worth nothing. And if you do this, we shall have been justly dealt with by you, both I and my sons" (Plato, *Great Dialogues*, trans. W. H. D. Rouse, New York 1970).

Paul's warning is blunt. Everyone who surrenders to false values distorts the image of Christ and cannot reveal God's inner harmony.

"If anyone thinks he is something when he is nothing, he deceives himself" (Gal 6:14).

3 False and true self limits

Pride can be a strait-jacket on potential. Family, tradition and race can all dictate that only certain possibilities are open to us for obeying God. The Oxford way or the Baptist way or the Anglican way can close us to what God is doing.

No one thought Jackie Pullinger was a suitable missionary. In *Chasing the Dragon* she tells how God called her to the gangs, heroin addicts and prostitutes of Hong Kong. False limits said no through road, but God had other plans.

Pride can also conceal our actual limits. Certain things are beyond our capacity. Others there is no time for. Some Christians lose sight of what God is offering them today behind a thousand dreams of what might have been: "What if I hadn't taken that job?" "Or if I hadn't married?" "Or if I hadn't joined that church?" "If you attempt to do all that is possible, all that is desirable, all that might be edifying, you will never succeed. Such an aim would indeed lack simplicity, humility and frankness" (A. de Tourville, *Letters of Spiritual Direction*, Oxford 1982).

There were plenty of things Jesus might have done on earth, but he didn't. He didn't do anything about Roman control of Israel. He didn't reform the worship of the synagogues. He didn't even take a professorship in Old

Testament studies to improve the standards of biblical scholarship! Jesus had a particular calling from God. So do we.

4 My world, my way

A baby learns quickly to suck for her milk and to cry if food doesn't come fast. Her world revolves around her own needs, just as surely as the earth revolves around the sun. "We are all born in moral stupidity, taking the world as an udder to feed our supreme selves" (George Eliot, *Middlemarch*).

Jesus turns our selfish instincts inside out. God comes first, then others, and last ourselves. What's more, "do as you would be done by" (Matt 7:12) doesn't mean treat everyone else as if they were you. We knew a family who, all except the mother, were fond of the hard centres in a box of chocolates. But the mother always ate the hard centres first, convinced that, by choosing what she liked least, she was doing everyone else a favour!

Jesus invites us to "stand in other people's shoes", to see the world as they see it, and to realise what is important for them. Wholeness comes through abandoning the baby's self-centredness. It comes through recognising others aren't only our equals but are each different to ourselves. And it comes through making them a higher priority than the baby's natural number one. "Do nothing out of selfish ambition or vain conceit, but in humility consider others better than yourselves. Each of you should look not only to your own interests, but also to the interests of others" (Phil 2:3–4).

5 False competition

The competitive drive is intense. Set several people the same problem and it will turn into a race. We compete to prove we are better than others. And we compete from our own insecurity: we are not sure we are worth very much, so we try to prove it through success.

Winners are rarely satisfied: they often rush to find

another competition. The rat-race isn't a modern invention for high-flying computerised careers. It is as old as man. Confucius advised his followers in the fifth century BC; "It is not the failure of others to appreciate your abilities that should trouble you, but rather your failure to appreciate theirs" (*Analects* 1:15, trans. D. C. Lau, London 1979).

Paul recognised the consuming power of this drive. He doesn't dismiss all ambition, but insists that any boasting must only be in "the cross of our Lord Jesus Christ" (Gal 6:14). Similarly, if we help a fellow Christian through some difficulty, we must never think ourselves immune to sin (Gal 6:1).

Christ wants us to be free from insecure competitiveness. Endlessly "comparing to somebody else" (Gal 6:4) is an unhealthy obsession. It destroys the harmony of the Spirit, within both the individual and the fellowship.

Self-assessment is valuable, but our measure is Christ. Wholeness concerns how much of Christ has been formed within. Wholeness doesn't need to keep measuring our progress against that of others.

There is no league table of the Holy Spirit in which we all compete. The one Spirit desires every Christian to grow in inner harmony in Christ.

No two ways

Radio phone-ins can be relied on for one thing: if two experts are in the studio, each caller will receive two quite different answers.

BBC's *Gardeners' Question Time* takes it further. One expert praises chemical additives. A second advises double digging, or something equally energetic. Then comes a third reply, full of Latin names for plants, recommending countless varieties in preference to the one the questioner is struggling to grow.

Up to date gardeners are all about trace elements and systemic insecticide. Traditionalists seem dedicated to muscular activity, unable even to enjoy their blooms without breaking into a sweat. But the scientist still needs his spade, just as no double digger can be complete without his bonemeal.

When it comes to the Spirit, Christians often slip into opposite camps. We might add that the incomprehensible third expert on gardening is like some modern preachers and theologians, living in a world unrecognisable to the rest of us!

What God has joined together, we divide. The Spirit is set in needless conflict with the Word or tradition with mind or matter. This risks dividing us from each other, from inner wholeness, and even from the Spirit. The problem isn't new. The New Testament tackles it for us.

1 Spirit and Word

Paul is quite clear. The Spirit breathed Scripture into life. That doesn't mean he dictated it, but every sentence of the Bible has double authorship, God and man. The same Spirit now makes Scripture unmistakably alive. He makes Scripture teach about God, rebuke our self-centredness, and train us in living for Jesus (2 Tim 3:16). The Spirit created the Bible, and he knew what he was doing. He won't contradict it.

Jesus taught the same. He promised the Spirit would remind the apostles of all he had taught. The gospels would depend on the living Spirit, not on mere human memory.

What's more, the Spirit would teach all things. He wouldn't shut up shop after Pentecost, but would explain why Jesus had to die. When the New Testament was complete, the Spirit didn't withdraw. In every generation, he lights up the Bible afresh. For every Christian, he gives inner witness that in the Bible, God has spoken.

David Smith used to warn in York, "If you have the Word without the Spirit, you dry up. If you have the Spirit without the Word, you blow up. But if you have both together, you grow up!"

The Spirit doesn't speak in a different voice to Scripture. But we need the Spirit's living presence to make Scripture more than a dead letter on the page. For the first Christians, the Spirit didn't replace the Old Testament. He made it more clear, more relevant, more practical and more alive than it had ever been before. If someone says the Spirit is saying something against the Bible, that is not the Spirit of God.

Most of us tend to jump to hasty conclusions. In his *Book of Martyrs* John Foxe told how Thomas Cranmer used a very different method to rediscover the truths of the Gospel: "When Martin Luther was risen up . . . before he would addict his mind to any opinion, he spent three whole years reading over the books of Holy Scripture."

Many centuries ago, a philosopher called Origen summed up to a young Christian how the Spirit and the Bible go together:

> Do you then, my son, diligently apply yourself to the reading of the sacred Scriptures. Apply yourself, I say. For we who read the things of God need much application, lest we should say or think anything too rashly about them . . . And applying yourself thus to the divine study, seek aright . . . for prayer is of all things indispensable to the knowledge of the things of God.

Spirit or Word? God has given both. And we need both.

2 Spirit and tradition

For many Christians, the authority of the Bible is clear for every generation. But what about tradition? In a world that is constantly changing, what is the value of yesterday's ideas? We hold fast to the promise that God is doing a new thing (Isa 43:18–19). We steer clear of churches stuck in the past. David Watson told a story of a man who had been a churchwarden for many years, who said ". . . and in all that time I've resisted every single change!" Those who live for the past are dead to the future. But if we ignore the past, we neglect its wisdom and are condemned to repeat its mistakes.

A local church had some rather unattractive late Victorian lettering on the front wall. You noticed it was old-fashioned more than what it actually said. But when it finally came to redecorating they would retouch it, "same as it has always been". Bad tradition eventually turns a church into a museum.

But in 1 Cor 11, Paul reveals a vital tradition. What the Lord had passed on to Paul, he has passed on to each local church, and now repeats to the Corinthians. This tradition is the words of the institution of the Lord's Supper, and ever since the words handed on to the Corinthians have been preserved and handed on to every church in every country in every age. In the same way, whatever translation we use, when we pray the Lord's Prayer we echo the prayer that Jesus gave, which has been used by his disciples in a living tradition in every generation.

The Spirit has always been present in Christ's Church. Just as he teaches us the meaning of Scripture, he has given rich insight to previous generations. The early Christians spoke of the Rule of Faith, in which the doctrine and practical instruction of the Bible was summed up. Our own Bible studies are never infallible, and nor is tradition. But tested against the Bible, we should expect the wisdom of past Christians to be "helpful as a guide, much more right than wrong" (Jim Packer, from an essay in *Scripture and Truth*, Grand Rapids 1983 – edited D. A. Carson and J. D. Woodbridge).

There are two problems. First what C. S. Lewis called "chronological snobbery". That means assuming that the latest is always the best. It is a common attitude in our fast-moving and proud modern culture. The book of Proverbs tells us to respect the wisdom of past generations. The Spirit invites us to hear his voice through their witness to Christ.

The second problem grew out of the Reformation. Because tradition had claimed for itself supreme authority, Luther had to confront it with Scripture. He reclaimed final authority for the gospel of grace. Ever since, some

Protestants, especially free church evangelicals, have swung to the opposite extreme: they assume tradition must always or almost always be wrong. Tradition is guilty unless proved innocent.

This raises a problem. If the Church has always misheard the Spirit in the past, how could we be sure of hearing him today?

In correcting tradition, Luther never dismissed the value of truly biblical insights from the past. The Christian who refuses to learn from the words and writings of others depends on his own pride more than on the Spirit. Jim Packer warns that, "one can point today to such groups whose interpretative style, though disciplined and conscientious, is narrow, shallow, naive, lacking in roots, and wooden to a fault, for want of encounter with the theological and expository wisdom of nineteen Christian centuries" (Jim Packer, *Scripture and Truth*, Grand Rapids 1983).

John Wesley refused to be tied down to traditional evangelistic methods. But at the same time he devoted much time, energy and money to republishing Christian classics. After Bible reading he encouraged regular study of the best Christian books of every age. They have been given to us by the goodness of God. Richard Foster's study guide to *Celebration of Discipline* provides invaluable up-to-date assistance to rediscover the old books through which the Spirit still speaks.

It's the same with hymns. Some seem to think that you can only worship God through hymns written before the war. (Sometimes before the Boer War.) Others think something is only "of the Spirit" if it was written since 1980.

Neither age nor youthfulness is any guarantee of true spirituality! Some old hymns are deadweight in the hymnbooks, and some modern songs are pretty dreadful. But the one Spirit has given fresh songs in every age. Some are useful only for a few years, but others stay full of life and zest for centuries.

We need to rejoice in all that the Spirit has given in the past, and in all that he is giving today. Only pride can presume to reduce true worship to *my* taste, and true wisdom to *my* generation.

In respecting the past, we respect our parents, and our forefathers. That isn't very fashionable, but it is the fifth commandment. The Spirit invites us to recognise that he has been guiding Christians in every generation. If we test the past by Scripture, we honour the Spirit. If we reject the past out of hand, we reject what the Spirit has done. In doing that, we reject him too.

3 Spirit and mind

Some Christians seem to suggest that the Holy Spirit makes the human brain redundant. Others almost seem to require a university entrance exam for conversion.

The Book of Proverbs walks a tightrope between underrating and overrating the human mind. Through searching and discipline a man can find wisdom (Prov 3:11–13). But he must not lean on his own understanding (Prov 3:5). True wisdom begins with the fear of the Lord, in whose presence intellectual pride is shown to be nonsense. Self-confidence is replaced by trust in the Lord, who gives his wisdom to the faithful.

It isn't that the mind is worthless. But it needs to be harnessed in humble service of God. When it claims to be self-sufficient and its own master, trouble is sure to follow.

John Newman faced this temptation while studying at Oxford. Later he wrote, "I was beginning to prefer intellectual excellence to moral; I was drifting . . ." Knowledge about God risked becoming more important than love for God. That would be disastrous, and he swiftly repented the fault. Learning was not evicted, but was made afresh the junior partner to Christian devotion.

When men and women rely on their minds alone, they create a god in their own image. A theology which is rooted in human pride cannot grow beyond dead theory. Paul warned the Ephesians, "No longer live as the Gentiles do, in the futility of their thinking" (Eph 4:17).

The same Paul who warned against idle speculation also

wrote the letter to the Romans. This contains the most detailed New Testament exploration of the meaning of the Gospel. In that context he urges, "be transformed in the renewing of your mind" (Rom 12:2).

To be sure, Paul refers to our basic attitudes and instincts, but also to our understanding. God in Christ can renew the whole mind, because in Christ he has redeemed the whole person.

Luther was converted through reading Romans, and he never grew tired of its stimulus to the Christian mind: "It can never be read or pondered too much, and the more it is dealt with the more precious it becomes, and the better it tastes . . ."

In 1 Corinthians, Paul explains that no one can fully know the thoughts of another. In the same way, the human mind on its own cannot understand the mind of God. Therefore, to the unbeliever, the gospel seems foolish.

However, the Spirit of God "searches all things, even the deep things of God" (1 Cor 2:10). He can reveal spiritual truths beyond the grasp of the unaided human mind. And he is given to Christians to bring those truths home: "so we may understand what God has freely given us" (1 Cor 2:12).

Paul stresses the limits of the human mind on its own. But he also stresses the renewal and transformation of the mind through the Spirit. Because God's Spirit is now within us, Paul can say that God is each Christian's "instructor on the inside". This means that together, "we have the mind of Christ" (1 Cor 2:16).

The Spirit is by no means just interested in academic theology, but we can never claim his support for being anti-intellectual. As John Stott appealed, "Dear friend, never denigrate truth! Never disdain theology! Never despise your mind! If you do, you grieve the Holy Spirit of Truth" (*The Bible Book for Today*, Leicester 1982).

Some early Christians found Paul's letters rather complicated, and 2 Peter is sympathetic to their difficulties: "His letters contain some things that are hard to understand, which ignorant and unstable people distort, as they do other Scriptures, to their own destruction" (2 Peter 3:16).

Because Paul is sometimes difficult doesn't mean he has stopped depending on the Spirit. But at the same time, those who find it a struggle to follow his arguments are by no means spiritually second rate.

I remember one Christian girl who had never been successful at school exams. Her minister was one of those brilliant people who could take extra A-levels for pleasure. Sadly she equated spirituality with brainpower, and thought she was somehow closer to God by struggling out of her depth in highbrow theology.

Jesus didn't say, "Go to university, suitable or not." He said, "Follow me." For some that will certainly mean further education. God wants you to use the brain he has given, depending on his Spirit. "All Christians are called to use their minds to the full . . . There is no substitute for hard work on the word of God" (Bruce Milne, *Know the Truth*, Leicester 1982).

If God has given you a first class brain, don't be reluctant to use it, but always make sure you depend on his Spirit. And if your brain-power is more average, thank God for it, and continue to exercise it for him, relying on the same Spirit.

John Donne wrote that truth stands, "On a huge hill, cragged and steep." The indispensable guide to truth's mountain is the Holy Spirit. But he agrees to assist all who confess Jesus as Lord, not just those with a sackful of degrees.

Spirit and mind? The one is given to enrich the other. The finest expression of this I have found is the prayer which John Calvin prayed before giving his lectures at Geneva: "May the Lord grant that we study the heavenly mysteries of his wisdom, making true progress in religion to his glory and our upbuilding. Amen."

4 Spirit and the matter

Israel's neighbours made up stories about creation in which a god of order waged war with a goddess of chaos. But Genesis 1 confirms that Yahweh is the only God. By him alone all things were made. And all that he made is good. That means God is interested in the natural world and the whole of life, not just the parts we sometimes think are "spiritual" or "religious". As C. S. Lewis put it, "God likes matter, he invented it."

The Corinthian Christians were into exotic spiritual experiences. If it was sensational, they wanted it. They really thought they had arrived. Paul had to remind them that the marks of the apostles were not success or spiritual highs so much as devotion to God and persecution. Spiritual living means, above all else, putting into practice the Sermon on the Mount – "We are fools for Christ . . . we are in rags, we are brutally treated, we are homeless, . . . when we are cursed, we bless; when we are persecuted, we endure it; when we are slandered, we answer kindly" (1 Cor 4:10–13).

The Corinthian problem went deeper. They were so concerned about things "spiritual", that they thought sin didn't really matter any more. They got involved in all kinds of degrading and foolish behaviour. What's more, just like their Greek neighbours, they looked forward to death as the moment when the soul escaped from the prison of the body.

Paul had to remind them that while the old and sinful nature must be crucified, God had saved their bodies as well as their souls. The temple of the Holy Spirit isn't otherworldly, it is the physical body of every Christian (1 Cor 6:19). What is more, just as Jesus was raised physically and left an empty tomb, beyond death we will receive a resurrection body (1 Cor 15:42–4). God didn't just make our bodies, he redeemed them.

The Colossians had a similar problem. They too tried to oppose the Spirit to matter. Some took delight in describing their visionary experiences at great length. Others got involved in some kind of mysterious angel worship

(Col 2:18). They were addicted to other-worldliness. Paul called this superspirituality a set of "idle notions" (Col 2:18).

Worse still, they combined their "hollow and deceptive ideas" (Col 2:8) with legalism. To free their souls for visions, they tied down their bodies with countless laws: "Do not handle! Do not taste! Do not touch!" (Col 2:21). Where the Corinthians indulged in lawlessness, the Colossians came into terrible legalistic bondage.

Paul would have none of it. He knew that "harsh treatment of the body" lacks "any value in restraining sensual indulgence" (Col 2:23). A heart change was needed, and that was what the Spirit offered. The Colossians needed to pray for practical renewal on the inside, and turn from their obsession with visions and angels.

To drive home his point, Paul considers the incarnation. The Colossians found bodies so distasteful that they began to think of Christ as a sort of spiritual apparition, without any real body at all. For Paul, this was unthinkable. He spells out the fully human and historical reality of Jesus who was also God: "In Christ all the fullness of the Deity lives in bodily form" (Col 2:9).

The Colossians had thought that Spirit and body were like oil and water. Paul reveals that not only does God save us fully, body and soul, but the Son of God took upon himself a fully human form.

This may all seem rather remote. But it has crucial implications. It means that God is involved in my everyday world, and not just the religious bits. It means that he is interested in washing up and gardening, as well as prayer and Bible study. It means that my work isn't less important to God if I am in business, rather than what is often mistakenly called "full time Christian work" – all suitable work can be full time Christian work: our highest calling is to become a Christian, *not* to become a clergyman or missionary.

Christian discipleship, therefore, includes a healthy diet and sufficient exercise. God is interested in sport, and

athletes may wish to request at least one part of the
experience of Samson:
"Then the Spirit of the Lord came upon him in power"
(Jud 14:19).

God is also interested in natural beauty, for the universe
he created declares his glory. This does mean, incidentally,
that a poster or painting of some beauty spot is thoroughly
Christian without the addition of an appropriate text. God
in his wisdom created the trees without Bible verses en-
graved automatically in their bark. They don't need words
to tell his glory.

Francis Bacon said God has given two books: the
Bible, the book of his words, and nature, the book of his
works. The scientist explores the mysteries of God's
handiwork.

Finally, it means that God is interested in art and im-
agination. Our creativity comes from the creator God, in
whose image we are made. What's more, Christians now
have within them the Spirit of the Creator. God can open
our eyes both to nature and to art. His spirit can release
our imaginations, and unlock a creativity we never knew
before.

Spirit and matter? They were brought into decisive
harmony in the incarnation. God invented matter and he
redeemed it. Every time we celebrate the Lord's Supper we
see them working together, for while the bread and wine
nourish us physically, we are invited also to "feed on
Christ, by faith, in our hearts, with thanksgiving".

The master craftsman

You may have been surprised at this chapter. I believe that
some Christians are rediscovering the power of the Spirit
without showing many signs of rediscovering inner wholeness. We have seen that God loves you and accepts you in
Christ just as you are, but self-acceptance is only the
beginning of our response. As Walter Trobisch wrote:
"God's love does not allow us to remain as we are. It is

more than mere acceptance" (*Love Yourself*, Baden-Baden 1976).

Paul brings the promise of wholeness to a memorable climax in the hymn to Christ in Colossians 1:15–20. Over creation and over the Church, Christ is agent, head and sustainer. *Agent* because by the one Christ we were both created and saved. *Head* because the one Christ is both Lord of creation and Head of his Church. *Sustainer* because the one Christ keeps everything going, both in the universe and in his new creation.

If you only think of Christ in narrowly religious terms, Paul tells you that your Christ is too small. In him all things hold together. Christ alone is our vision and our hope of true harmony and wholeness.

Michelangelo was once offered a huge block of marble. It was so terribly flawed that all the artists in Florence had abandoned it as unusable. But Michelangelo said he could already see the finished statue, imprisoned within the crudely hewn and damaged block.

Three years later the magnificent and noble figure of David was revealed to an astonished world. To see it takes your breath away and leaves you lost for words. To think that something so perfect should have been carved from marble that had once seemed quite worthless!

We have considered the fragments and inner contradictions of our own flawed lives. We may sometimes seem to ourselves quite worthless. But God is the master craftsman. He wants to shape and restore each of us, setting free each Christian as someone unique, and whole, and beautiful.

The New Testament shows the Spirit's gift of wholeness to be inclusive and patient. We need to rediscover that inclusiveness, and reclaim Christ as the Lord of the whole of life, holding all things together. But we should never expect complete wholeness overnight. "It is right that you should begin again every day. There is no better way to finish the spiritual life than to be ever beginning it over again, and never to think that you have arrived" (Francis de Sales).

8

NEW HARMONY — GIFTS FOR THE BODY

One of the most exciting quarterbacks today is Jim McMahon. When he is at his best, the Chicago Bears head for sensational victories. A good quarterback takes chances when the game offers him opportunities. But a great quarterback makes chances out of nothing. Before a pass looks possible, the ball bullets to a wide receiver. Touchdowns are made to look easy.

At the height of their careers, top players are worth their weight in gold. Crowds cheer them, autograph hunters lie in wait for them, and coaches try every trick they know to buy them. In sports clubs across the country, countless high schoolers dream of playing as skillfully as Dan Marino, Terry Bradshaw, Joe Montana, and other sporting superstars.

But suppose the dreams of these high schoolers came true and hundreds of the latest stars were reproduced. The bottom would drop out of the transfer market. One Dan Marino may be magnificent, two could be even better, but pity the coach whose entire team had exactly the same skills and exactly the same temperament. A team comprised of McMahons and Refrigerators would not be very effective.

Of course, it's different for some sports, like rowing, where the ideal crew rows in perfect harmony with almost identical action. But the most popular team sports, both to watch and to play, are usually those where you work as a team, but don't lose sight of individual skills.

Paul recognised it was the same with the human body and the Church. It is precisely because there are so many different parts, with so many different functions, that the human body can do so much and is so adaptable. When Paul calls the Church a body, he has in mind not an out of condition "armchair spectator" but a well-trained athlete. Everything is in top condition and doing its work to the full.

Sadly, the Church often seems more like a bus than a body. Everyone slumps back passively in the pews except the "professional" in the driving seat at the front, who "does it all".

Gifts for the body

Paul writes about the body of Christ in four letters: 1 Corinthians, Romans, Colossians, and Ephesians. He describes the Church in many other ways, including the new family, the Bride of Christ, and the new temple which is founded on Christ and filled with his Spirit. But "the body of Christ" seems his favourite way of describing the Church.

Body-talk isn't just a pep talk for divided fellowships. Paul doesn't dream up this comparison simply to inject some team spirit into the Corinthians. It's not that the Church at its best functions something like a body. By baptism and profession of faith we actually become part of the united body of Christ. The gift of the Spirit makes us one:

". . . we were all given the one Spirit to drink" (1 Cor 12:13).

This is crucial. If the Spirit was only given at a later stage than conversion, only those who had received him could be linked by him into Christ's body. Of course, that is not to say that conversion is the Spirit's last active moment in Christians.

Imagine a body made up entirely of eyes, or a body in the shape of a single big toe. It might make a wonderful puppet for children's television, but would be useless in the real world.

Sometimes everyone in a church wants to be like the minister. But Paul stops us short. The Church isn't meant to produce ρew upon pew of carbon-copy look-alikes. It isn't unfortunate that we are all different. It's God's intention.

God's ideal for the Church is a very mixed assortment. This doesn't mean a rag-bag of isolated individuals, each doing their own thing. Fellowship is like a symphony: out of many different instruments a beautiful harmony grows. Every snowflake is unique. How much more does God care for each individual Christian as he builds us together in the new family of love.

God intends us all to be different, and he gives us different functions. Each Olympics pushes back the frontiers of human achievement. What was beyond reach at Rome had become necessary in some events at Los Angeles just for a place in the final. The slow motion shots of gold medal performances celebrate the body's potential in peak condition.

Different events need different physiques. Some years ago the Russians were meant to have found their gold medal sprinter, Borzhov, by asking a computer to discover the ideal physical requirements for the 100 metres. Over 5,000 metres Borzhov would have fared no better against Brendan Foster than Zola Budd shot-putting against the giantesses of Eastern Europe. Not even Daley Thompson is equally good at every event.

We have to find our particular God-given strengths. No one has ever received every gift of the Spirit, just as no one is equipped for every sport. In the Winter Olympics of 1984, the world watched entranced as Jayne Torvill and Christopher Dean danced the Bolero. They were in a class of their own. Perfect scores were almost guaranteed.

Meanwhile, one of the less glamorous events was in progress. This was the single sled, or luge, in which you race down the steeply curving ice track, cornering at speeds which would be lethal on level ground in a car. You lie face down a few inches above the ice, on a tiny sled which is the only thing between you and certain disaster. To compete at all a certificate of insanity helps.

tory in the women's event went to an East German.

She was the ideal shape for staying on the sled at maximum speed. In fact she had a weighty advantage over the competition, being a burly 13 stone.

I couldn't resist imagining the lady of the luge partnering Christopher Dean in the Bolero! No one can do everything. If anyone tries to do everything in the Church, not least the minister, we are courting disaster.

We finally need to add that when each role is different, not all of them will be equally glamorous. It's the same in soccer: a Kevin Keegan or Bobby Robson will be in the thick of the action for ninety minutes. If his team is on top, a goalie may only need to make two or three saves in a whole match. He needs the character to wait alone in his area, concentrating on the game at the other end of the pitch, always prepared for that vital moment when he alone can keep the ball out.

Athletics is now glamorous big business. Mary Decker and Tessa Sanderson have been cover-girls on topselling magazines. It wasn't their good looks that made them sporting superstars, but glamour is seen in a smiling face.

I can't remember a TV feature on a top runner's toes. Yet without toes we couldn't balance properly, let alone sprint. It's the same in the Church: not every ministry is up front in the public eye. The backroom jobs, often done so efficiently they are not even noticed, are just as vital.

Paul insists there is no need for anyone in the Church to feel worthless. Not only did Christ consider each one worth dying for, he has even given every single Christian at least one special gift. Every single member of the body of Christ is needed. In fact Paul goes further: every Christian is indispensable.

What kind of gifts?

Whenever Paul teaches about the body, he links it to three things: the gifts of the Spirit, the centrality of love, and the pattern of Christian worship. Gifts, love and worship are only possible through the Spirit. He has the power to make "the body of Christ" a living reality, experienced in practice, and not just wishful thinking.

The gifts of the Spirit are enormously varied. The Spirit simply will not be tied down to any rigid formula. Traditional Pentecostals counted nine gifts in 1 Cor 12:8–10, and claimed this was Paul's definitive list. These are gifts of knowing (discernment, wisdom and knowledge), gifts of doing (healing, miracles and faith) and gifts of speech (prophecy, tongues and interpretation). All these gifts are certainly in this list, although the sorting into three groups is not done by Paul. But there are in fact two other lists of gifts within this one chapter.

The first list, as above, follows Paul's reaffirmation that while the gifts are diverse, they come from the one and only Spirit of God. The second list sums up Paul's argument that each Christian has at least one particular gift within the one body (1 Cor 12:28). He omits discernment, wisdom, knowledge, faith and interpretation, and adds instead the gift of administration, together with apostles and teachers.

In this list Paul mixes descriptions of the gift – "those having gifts of . . ." – with a name for what those with certain gifts do in the Church – apostles rather than those with apostolic gifts, and the same for prophets, teachers and workers of miracles. Paul doesn't suggest that these four are official positions in every Church that someone has to be slotted into, like so many places on the PCC or eldership. On the contrary, they are gifts under the control of the Spirit. But there does seem to be something special about them.

Paul begins this second list with an order of priority for the first three or four, but then stops numbering them. This seems to suggest that although some gifts of key leadership are obvious, you really cannot count up every spiritual gift, let alone try to set every gift in some kind of order.

The third list (1 Cor 12:29–30) contains seven gifts. The first five from the second list are retained, together with tongues. Interpretation of tongues is reinserted, but administration goes unmentioned. This list is composed as

SPIRITUAL GIFTS

1 Cor 12:8–10	1 Cor 12:28	1 Cor 12:29	Rom 12:6–8	Eph 4:11
	apostles	apostles		apostles
	prophets	prophets	prophesying	prophets
	teachers	teachers	teaching	pastors–teachers
wisdom				
knowledge				
faith				
gifts of healing	gifts of healing	gifts of healing		
miraculous powers	workers of miracles	workers of miracles		
prophecy*				
discerning spirits				
different tongues	different tongues	tongues		
interpreting tongues		interpretation		
	helping others		serving	
	administration		encouraging	
			contributing to needs of others	
			leadership	
			showing mercy	
				evangelists

* Prophecy comes sixth in the first list, but is second in all the others.

a series of questions. The Corinthians must all have been hankering after the same gifts, because the questions are phrased to invite the same answer. Paul spells it out for us. Is every member given the same gifts? Of course not!

These three lists alone are enough to prove that the Spirit delights in variety. If we turn to that in Romans 12:6–8, we find once again that it follows a description of the one body in which different members have different functions. What's more, just as 1 Corinthians 13 makes love central to any discussion of the body and the gifts, the second half of Romans 12 centres on Christian love.

This list records eight gifts: prophecy, serving, teaching, encouraging, contributing to the needs of others, and showing mercy. Seven of these eight don't appear in the first list in 1 Corinthians 12. All but prophecy and teaching don't appear in the earlier chapter at all.

There is no indication that Paul is listing only the gifts exercised in the Church at Rome. Nor does he suggest that this or any other list contains the most important gifts.

About twenty seven different gifts have been found in the New Testament. God has lavished upon us the riches of his grace (Eph 1:7–8) and the unsearchable riches of Christ (Eph 3:8). With such love beyond limit, an exhaustive list of spiritual gifts is clearly impossible.

One feature of the list in Romans 12 is particularly striking. Paul keeps the gift of leadership well away from the gifts of teaching and prophecy. Not every leader is a gifted teacher, and the teacher need not claim the authority to lead. In fact, Paul seems to suggest that a teacher may well benefit from working under the leadership of others.

So often in our churches supreme leadership is in the hands of the one or two man-band of "professionals", who do most of the teaching and also most of the leading. According to Paul, there is no automatic connection between these gifts.

A man may be an excellent teacher, but a mediocre leader, or vice versa. To recognise this is by no means an admission of failure. Failure is when someone pretends they have got gifts God has withheld, is too proud to admit he is human, and prevents others who have got those gifts from exercising them. It may even be that God deliberately withholds certain key gifts from many "professional" clergy, to try to force their hand towards a humble dependence on others in every member ministry.

This is parallelled in 1 Corinthians 14 concerning the prophets. It seems that many Christians will prophesy occasionally, but there are others for whom this is a regular ministry. This smaller group is then termed the prophets. They lead the Church in discerning whether a particular prophecy is from the Lord. But this does not mean they automatically have a wider leadership role.

No one should try to exploit a gift like teaching or prophecy to try to obtain power or authority in the Church. The Spirit is quite capable of giving the distinctive gift of Christian leadership.

Gifts of leadership

Paul concentrates in Ephesians 4 upon the different gifts that make up local church leadership. There is absolutely no suggestion, here or anywhere else in the New Testament that God intends local leadership to be in the hands of a single person. Christian leadership is plural leadership.

This means much more than one man delegating certain tasks while keeping hold of all the reins of power, and retaining in his own hands total control. Plural leadership means leadership that is shared, not merely tasks that are handed over. David Watson used to submit all his invitations to speak to the eldership in York, and *together* they would discern the mind of Christ for his wider ministry.

Five gifts are listed: apostles, prophets, evangelists, pastors and teachers (Eph 4:11). Notice that, once again, the only consistent ordering concerns apostles and prophets. Wherever these two gifts are both listed, they always come first.

Two meanings are commonly recognised for the gift

of apostleship. First, the foundational eye-witnesses, appointed once-for-all by Christ, to provide the decisive leadership and permanent authoritative teaching for the Church in every generation. Paul is added to the original apostles as the special apostle to the Gentiles, "as one untimely born".

The second meaning is the church planter who breaks new ground after the pattern of Paul's missionary enterprise. In this sense, Barnabas (Acts 14:4, 14; 1 Cor 9:5–6), James the Lord's brother (Gal 1:19), Silas (1 Thess 2:6) and Andronicus and Junias (Rom 16:7) are all termed apostles. In this second sense, there is always an abundant need for church planters, not least today in the so-called Christian countries of Western Europe. Any church planting role needs always to be kept carefully distinct from the once-for-all, unique authority and teaching of the first generation apostles.

We will consider prophecy at length in a later chapter. For now we simply need to note that the New Testament, just like the Old, does not restrict it to predictions about the future. Rather than foretelling, it means the telling forth of a particular word of God, with relevance to the immediate context and congregation.

As for the three remaining gifts, it is generally agreed that pastor and teacher go together. In some degree, you cannot be a real teacher without getting alongside people and genuinely caring for them. Similarly, someone with a caring ministry will naturally be providing some teaching as part of his comfort to those in need. There is no justification for "picking and choosing", so that the person who prefers books to people buries himself in his study and only comes out to preach at a congregation. If Jesus is our example, then every good teacher must first become a good listener.

Some, however, are much better pastors than teachers, and vice versa. Each needs to hear the Spirit guiding not only through the gifts he has given, but also through those withheld.

Finally we should note the importance given to evangelism as a distinct gift in this list. Evangelism isn't a once every few years obligation. The Spirit is a spirit of mission, and the Church is called to a life of mission. This suggests some evangelistic impact to every service, perhaps together with regular evangelistic guest services, given suitably attractive titles, invitation cards and posters, plenty of notice to invite friends, an imaginative and uncomplicated order of service, and most important, special prayer meetings.

Once again, it is not obligatory that any one pastor or teacher should lay claim to a monopoly of evangelistic gifts. In many contexts, someone with, for example, a career in the commercial world will have far more credibility than a clergyman. Not many ministers' life stories could become a bestselling paperback. Such books can have evangelistic impact in parts few clergy ever reach.

King Arthur's round table had one place that none but the most perfect knight dare claim, on pain of instant death. Some pulpits are guarded so jealously they would appear to threaten the same fate to any preacher who is not ordained!

The purpose of these gifts of leadership is quite clear: "to prepare God's people for works of service" (Eph 4:12). It is not the minister who does all the ministering. Leaders are appointed by the Spirit to release the gifts of every other member.

Leaders are essential not because without them "ministry" cannot be undertaken, but because they are the key enablers, identifying and drawing out the gifts of others. A good leader is sorely missed when he moves, but ministry continues in his absence. A poor leader may also be sorely missed, but if ministry revolved around his particular gifts, without him the fellowship crumbles.

Christian ministry, according to Ephesians 4, is essentially corporate. As the Spirit bestows gifts, God's people minister to one another. In this way the body of Christ is enriched. As the body grows, the fellowship grows *together* in unity of faith and in knowing Christ as Lord and Saviour (Eph 4:12–13).

Many churches in an "interregnum" (I don't think Paul would like that word at all!) long for the arrival of the next minister, and look forward to his ministry among them. How much more, according to Paul, do we need to long for the release of the gifts of every member.

The Strongest Man in Europe competition has one hugely muscled man dragging along a two-ton truck. Muscles and veins seem fit to burst as the truck inches forward and the seconds tick away. Paul writes of "every supporting ligament" (Eph 4:16) and the body "supported and held together by its ligaments and sinews" (Col 2:19). His vision is certainly not of some heroic minister, sinews stretched to the limit, dragging behind him a vast, unwieldy, passive congregation.

Five keys to spiritual gifts

We need to note five key principles about spiritual gifts:

1 The Spirit is not restricted to spectacular gifts
The various lists mix together gifts which grow out of natural aptitudes, like teaching or administration, with those like healing or tongues, which seem much less predictable. John Owen, the seventeenth century Puritan who was Vice Chancellor of the University of Oxford, summed up most helpfully these two kinds of gifts: gifts "such as consisted in extraordinary improvements of the faculties of the minds of men" and gifts "such as exceeded all the powers and faculties of men's minds" (*Pneumatologia* quoted in John Stott, *Baptism and Fullness*, Leicester 1975).

We need to recognise that the church administration and finances depend as much as, for example, a ministry of healing, on the gifts of the Spirit. There is nothing worse than leaving the Spirit out of day to day affairs, as if we can cope there by ourselves, or as if he's a far removed managing director, who really doesn't want to be troubled with mundane details. This doesn't mean natural gifts can be ascribed casually to the Spirit, but it does mean we can offer him "what comes naturally", and ask him to enrich and transform it.

We should be very careful about lists of selected spiritual gifts. I saw recently a list of nine: pastoral, teaching, preaching, evangelism, administration, healing, practical help, service to society, and leadership. You marked which was your strength, and it went on the central church file.

The intentions were good, and it will probably be useful in practice, but it raised three problems:

a) It looked like being above all a way of getting "volunteers" more easily. ("You said this is your gift, so here's your chance to use it!")
b) It blurred the line between natural aptitude and spiritual gifts, apparently not recognising that, as with shy Timothy, God can give gifts way outside our natural capabilities.
c) It was a very selective list. So many kinds of New Testament gift are missed out that it seems written more with a view to what the leaders wanted in a Church than what the Spirit might choose to give.

2 There is no league table of spiritual gifts

The gifts which grow out of natural aptitudes are no less given by the Spirit and no less important to the Church than the others. There is no rigid division between a "spiritual" part of life, and a "secular" part. Whether the Spirit grants a new gift or empowers a natural aptitude, the gift in action is always something very special. "When God uses a person's gifts, it is anything but natural" (E. Schweizer, *The Holy Spirit*, London 1980).

The Spirit is concerned with every part of the life of the Church, and he is involved in every activity of individual Christians.

3 There is no distinct group of gifts granted only for the apostolic generation

All kinds of gifts are mixed in together. There even seems

overlap between some gifts, for example between preaching and teaching, or between gifts of wisdom and gifts of knowledge.

The only reference to **any gifts** passing away is in 1 Corinthians 13. Here, Paul says the gifts will cease at the same time as partial knowledge passes away. At that time, perfection comes and the imperfect disappears; we will see face to face instead of a poor reflection; and we shall know God fully, even as we are already known. There is only one time this could be: Paul uses the word *teleios* which he uses elsewhere to mean the perfect which will come at the end of time.

The New Testament cannon contain all the *essential* teaching for this life. But it doesn't answer all our questions and is by no means exhaustive. Only after Christ's second coming shall we finally see face to face. The time of perfect and complete knowledge of God is not yet.

All the spiritual gifts are intended, at the gracious discretion of God, for every generation. The spiritual gifts are for the Church on earth, not for those raised to eternal life.

4 Paul instructs us to "eagerly desire spiritual gifts"
There is no suggestion in the New Testament that we should keep on living as if the gifts don't exist, and simply leave it to God whether to give them. When the Thessalonians poured cold water on the gift of prophecy they were sternly rebuked by Paul: to despise spiritual gifts means to "put out the Spirit's fire" (1 Thess 5:19–20).

There is nothing wrong with desiring a spiritual gift, so long as we want to use it for the Church, and not for our own glory. In fact Paul particularly encourages the Corinthians to desire the gift of prophecy (1 Cor 14:1). How can they reasonably do this unless they request the gift in prayer?

We don't say it is presumption to pray that we might be born again. An earthly father delights to hear the requests of his children. How much more does our heavenly Father desire to hear our requests, especially when he has revealed that he delights to shower his gifts upon his church.

One well known preacher is said to have prayed earnestly for the gift of evangelism for three solid months. He became one of the most greatly used evangelists of his generation.

Of course, to ask is not the same as to demand. Earthly fathers don't take too kindly to being endlessly pestered with requests for more presents. To ask humbly is right and proper: to try to insist is always foolish.

Our heavenly Father reserves the right to know better than us what gifts we need. He also reserves the right to say, "No, my child": ". . . he gives them to each one, just as he determines" (1 Cor 12:11).

5 Once given, the gifts need care and effort

Spiritual gifts are not like switching to auto-pilot. Paul was certain that a particular gift had been given to Timothy. But Timothy was naturally shy. A powerful ministry in the public eye went right against his natural temperament.

The gift was burning less brightly, and may have been a little neglected, but Paul doesn't doubt it is still present. He urges Timothy to make every effort, in the Spirit of "power, love and self-discipline" (2 Tim 1:7). He needs to concentrate on the gift God gave and "fan it into flame" (2 Tim 1:6).

We are responsible for the use of the gifts God has given. Sometimes a gift may be given for a particular moment and then withdrawn. But if the decision to withdraw the gift is ours, not the Spirit's, we are playing with fire. Like Timothy, we need to stoke up our spiritual embers, and blaze anew to the glory of God.

Needing each other

The minister who took our marriage service gave some very useful advice. He said it was important always to treat your partner as someone very special. Otherwise, with passing years, someone once loved deeply can begin to feel treated like another piece of furniture. One suggestion he made was to make a habit of surprising each other with little gifts. Such love-gifts are just one way of keeping a relationship fresh and growing.

Often parents surprise their young children with love-gifts. The child's delight is worth more than words can say! But as children become more knowing, presents start to become expected. A surprise is anticipated by a demand. At that stage parents begin to worry quite rightly about spoiling the child. Gradually the supply of presents dries up.

Many adults only expect presents at Christmas and birthdays. In some jobs, Christmas presents from friends and family can seem almost swamped by the "gifts" from companies investing in your good will.

Most of us aren't very good at either giving or receiving presents. If someone so much as compliments us, we try to shrug it off – "Oh, it was nothing!" And if someone gives us a present, we wonder what might be the catch.

Just as salvation is a gift from God, he delights to shower his adopted children with love-gifts. The gifts of the Spirit are called *charismata*, which means gifts of grace. God doesn't provide his gifts as a perk for dedicated service or a reward for being religious. He doesn't give gifts because we deserve them or because our birthday has come round. He gives gifts, quite simply because he loves us.

Kidlington is the fastest growing village in England. That's nothing to be proud about, but it does mean our buses are crammed full. Recently two people sitting next to me in a tightly packed bus began talking about spiritual gifts. I must admit my ears pricked up.

The girl had recently prayed in tongues for the first time. She found the gift greatly enriched her prayer life, but she had a problem. Far from tongues making her arrogant, she thought her friend Mandy far more "committed" than she was. So why had God given her the gift, when Mandy was far more deserving?

We need to drive home the New Testament message time and again. The gifts of the Spirit are never a reward. Spiritual gifts are never God's stamp of approval on good works or attempts at self-improvement. We never ascend a league table of spiritual gifts and experiences, according to how well we are progressing. Paul says we have different gifts, not according to some merit table, but "according to the grace given us" (Rom 12:6). God's gifts are always love-gifts.

The early Church was very strange. People of startlingly different backgrounds mixed together. Jews would not allow Gentiles into the main temple areas, for they would defile the sacred place. Yet Jews and Gentiles were united in the New Israel. Slaves were someone else's possession, yet they worshipped alongside freemen and slave owners in the new family of the Father. Jewish men thanked God in regular prayer that they hadn't been born as women. Yet men and women became equal in Christ. All needed saving just as much. And all could be united in Christ.

It wasn't always easy. Paul urged the Roman Christians not to let the world "squeeze you into its mould" (Rom 12:2 J. B. Phillips). Deep rooted attitudes and prejudices need inner transformation through the Spirit's renewing power. The attitude Paul tackles first, in the very next verse, is pride: "Do not think of yourself more highly than you ought, but rather think of yourself with sober judgment, in accordance with the measure of faith God has given you" (Rom 12:3).

One side of this is snobbery. Later Paul urges the Romans to "be willing to associate with people of low position" (Rom 12:16). The one who conforms to the world, clings to the things that make him, in his own eyes, superior to others: nationality, colour, job, background, education, wealth, athleticism, or even how long you've been a Christian. Some were thinking too highly of themselves.

148

"I do wish the slaves would hold their own service."

"Wouldn't want Gentiles like that living in *our* neighbourhood."

Paul had to remind them that their only true status was "sinners saved by Christ".

Before Paul turns to social division, he looks first, immediately after verse three, at gifts in the church. The one who conforms to the world exploits the gifts he has been given to boost his own status and maximise his own advantage. Some were clearly thinking too highly of their gifts, treating them as their personal property:

"My gifts are really spectacular and showy!"

"I'd like to see this church try to get by without *me*!"

Paul confirms that different members have different gifts. But there is no link between particular gifts and any claim to special status. In the first century church, there was no top table for VIPs.

Any gift is a potential target for pride. The answer isn't for the Spirit to avoid giving gifts, but for our basic attitudes to be transformed. To the Corinthians, Paul makes the same point three times over to stress the great variety of gifts from the single divine giver. There are various kinds of gifts, various kinds of service, and various kinds of working, but there is only one Spirit, one Lord and one God (1 Cor 12:4–6).

Paul also stresses three times that every Christian is given at least one gift and some special task in the local fellowship:

"*to each one* the manifestation of the Spirit is given" (1 Cor 12:7).

"God has arranged the parts in the body, *every one of them*, just as he wanted them to be" (1 Cor 12:18).

"Now you are the body of Christ, and *each one of you* is part of it" (1 Cor 12:27).

So much repetition makes it quite clear that Paul is insisting on an essential characteristic of the new community which goes right against the grain of self-interest and conformity to the world. A spiritual gift doesn't belong to *me*. It is not given for *my* well-being. It belongs to the church, and is simply entrusted to me for safekeeping. Every spiritual gift is "given for the common good" (1 Cor 12:7).

It's not just the gifts that belong to the whole body. Each Christian is part of the body (1 Cor 12:27). Each Christian has a special function in the body (1 Cor 12:18). And because we form one body, Paul can even say that "each member *belongs to all the others*" (Rom 12:5). As a result, far from looking up to a social elite, or those with a particular gift, all members of the body "should have *equal concern* for each other" (1 Cor 12:25).

This is quite shattering for our commuter-style churches, where we sit in our regular places, making our private communion with God, with barely a word for our fellow worshippers, let alone any strangers. It's not just that we need each other in the sense of needing someone to take the collection, or needing someone to serve the coffee. An isolated Christian, whether refusing to take part in public worship or left on their own in their "private pew", is, according to the New Testament, a Christian who is incomplete.

The community of the Spirit is the place of new belonging. We shouldn't just make each other welcome. We need to discover in practice what it actually means to "belong to all the others". Interdependence isn't a mark of inadequacy. It is a hallmark of the body of Christ.

To sum up, all have something special to give. No one is superfluous. All are different. In fact the Spirit increases our natural diversity, by giving different gifts, to bring us not to clubbish conformity but to the true unity of interdependence.

All need to exercise their gifts, and so need opportunities to give. We need to be not just humble enough, but ready and eager to receive from every member. If we don't give, or if we try to give when we don't have the gifts, all suffer. If you don't let someone else give, all miss out. If you desire to do everything, you are quite mistaken. If you think you have nothing to offer, you are just as mistaken.

Paul makes it indisputably clear that Christians need each other. To fall out of spiritual dependence on each other is to fall back into old habits of isolation, and to let the world squeeze us back into its mould.

Learning to belong

Gifts need to be discovered. Opportunities have to be found not only for gifts to be exercised but for new gifts to be tried out. That means a caring context, where individuals are free to make mistakes, and where we can receive gentle correction, without feeling crushed or rejected.

In many churches, the central Sunday services are simply too large for everyone to take an active part, or for this kind of loving development of spiritual gifts. As David Prior's *The Church in the Home* argues so persuasively, this is where home groups come into their own. We need to note a few key principles:

1 Structure
Groups need to be small enough for a network of close, caring relationships to develop. Most studies recommend between seven and twenty members. Less or more than that and some will start to clam up.

Groups should generally be geographical, to increase possibilities of real mutual support. They need to meet weekly if possible, or at least fortnightly. A group that meets monthly has more or less to start a network of relationships all over again at each meeting. Prayer needs are often out of date or forgotten after a gap of four weeks. What's more, it often means that the parents of a young family each get to a group meeting just once every eight weeks.

In some circles great stress is laid on inter-church home groups. These may well be useful at a particular time of the year, say for a Lent course. The Body of Christ includes the worldwide church and not just your local fellowship. However, if home groups are a key starting point for putting into practice the New Testament vision of the local church, their first purpose is not for inter-church cooperation. Their first purpose is to let the local church be the church, by rediscovering how to belong to one another, to minister gifts to one another, and to experience in practice being the body of Christ.

2 Content

A home group Bible study should seek to involve everyone. Groups are not the best place for a lecture or sermon. Leading relaxed discussion which actually gets somewhere and doesn't lose sight of the text takes great skill and practical training. Some preachers are too talkative and dominant to be good home group leaders.

Prayer needs to be for each other, and not just for the church sick list. Of course those on such a list need prayer, but there are some home groups where it would seem almost indecent if someone asked for prayer for themselves unless their problem was probably terminal. Prayer for each other is not meant to be an act of last resort, when self-sufficient isolation finally breaks down.

A home group without songs of worship has lost a great deal. It is worth searching out secretive but gifted pianists and guitarists. It is also worth avoiding homes for group meetings where there are youngsters who sleep lightly!

The groups are always a complement to Sunday worship, never a substitute. Wider group responsibilities, within and beyond the church, help prevent them becoming too isolated or inward looking.

3 Leaders

Leaders need regular training and support, in a group which functions like the individual cell groups, containing the same number of people. The leaders' meeting should not be dominated by administration, nor chaired like a business meeting. The style of this meeting will greatly influence the style of individual groups.

If spiritual gifts are to be developed, training is needed in discernment. It may be worth visiting another church to see unfamiliar spiritual gifts in action. In addition, Scripture Union provide some excellent books and courses on how to make the most of home groups.

4 Problems

Some groups never seem to get off the ground. It is no good flogging a dead horse. All that achieves is to make the Christians who live in that area feel guilty or second-rate. Give a group time and prayer, but always remember that people matter more than structures. Better to dissolve that group into others that are firing on all cylinders.

It may be best for the youth group to have its own home group network. In one church a large youth group spontaneously started their own home groups. After a few years a directive came from on high that it would be much better for teenagers to join the adult groups. In practice, teenagers often felt out of place, unable to discuss their own needs and problems or contribute freely to Bible study. At the same time, some adults felt less able to share painful personal needs with their children's friends present.

Within a few months, a flourishing set of teenage home groups which would feed people into the adult groups in due course, was replaced by a handful of the most determined teenagers, doggedly sticking to adult groups where they didn't feel quite at home. Separate groups may not be needed in all circumstances, but our structures need considerable flexibility for personal and local needs.

5 Breakthroughs

The potential for home groups is enormous. Recent studies suggest that a church with one full-time minister normally reaches a ceiling of growth at about 150 members. Home groups are the best way to sustain real growth in depth, whether you have one, three or thirty full-time workers.

A group can achieve a breakthrough when someone takes the risk of making themselves very vulnerable. One group took off when a couple confided that they had been trying to have a baby for some ten years. The latest operation had gone wrong, and the doctors had given up all hope. They still longed for a baby, and asked the group to pray for them. A new kind of trust, openness and love began to flower throughout the group. As it happens, that couple now have two lovely children.

Another group discovered new depths when an elderly man prayed a one sentence prayer of confession. With tears in his eyes he murmured, "Dear Lord, only you know what we are really like." Suddenly everyone's defences were down. There was a shared experience of forgiveness, love for each other and open dependence on the Spirit of Christ. No one had to pretend anymore.

Being a Christian doesn't mean survival of the fittest. It means seeing each other as frail earthen vessels, yet recognising the treasure of Christ within (2 Cor 4:7). Learning to belong means learning together to be the body of Christ. Regular house groups are invaluable for exploring the spiritual gifts and for rediscovering the living reality of the "fellowship of the Holy Spirit".

The minister in the body

David Watson warned that the minister is so often the cork in the bottle, holding back the renewal of a local church. I am firmly convinced that, in many churches, the rekindling of body-fellowship and the practice of spiritual gifts depend on the leaders stepping aside from the rigid patterns of traditional ministry.

Rediscovering the body of Christ can bring great liberation to fulltime ministers. But it can also bring great strain. One minister raised the possibility of every member ministry and was firmly rebuked by his deacons: "But that's what

154

we pay you for!'' Another church's lay leaders proposed every member ministry and the minister was outraged: "But I've been trained and ordained to do those things. They are *my* patch!''

Many ministers have been trained to live as if they were able to meet every need in the local church. He alone, or along with fellow ministers, will make key decisions, lead all worship, preach every Sunday and do all the official counseling. For an older generation, the need for omni-competence was quite explicit at theological college. Today it still seeps unspoken into attitudes and ways of seeing "my ministry.''

If someone approaches his minister to suggest certain lay people may be better at some tasks, it isn't just hackles of pride that may rise. Such comments can seem to threaten a whole ministry. If a man has had ingrained through a lifetime that the minister should be omnicompetent, any suggestion that others may have gifts he lacks seems to question his whole calling and even his value as a minister. He may feel hurt and rejected. We need to love ministers out of their isolation and secret vulnerability.

The laity or *laos* is the whole people of God. Full-time ministry is a special calling within the people of God, not a separate and superior caste. Recently I met the new minister at the church where one of our friends has been active for years. "So you're the new minister at Clive's church,'' I said, meaning to be friendly. The reply was a brush-off, "I prefer to think of Clive as being a member of *my* church.'' "*My* church'' and "*my* people'' set a minister over against ordinary Christians.

Ministers can become a world apart, living a "proper'' Christian life in their "full-time Christian work.'' This can lead to clerical snobbery. It also causes "lay people'' to feel that God lets off the rest of us with half-measures of holiness. The New Testament doesn't allow different stand-ards either side of ordination. As J. N. D. Kelly, the early Church specialist noted: "the whole conception of double standards in basic Christian living was a later intrusion, and represented a falling away from the primitive ideal. All Christians alike . . . were expected to manifest the same spirit . . ." (*Aspects of the Passion*, Oxford 1985).

John Owen was quite clear that, in the New Testament, leadership gifts come direct from the Spirit. Gifts of ministry don't "come with the job", attached automatically to the office of clergyman through the rite of ordination. That doesn't deny the value of ordination, but reveals a misuse. "The Church has no power to call any person to the office of the ministry, where Christ hath not gone before it in the designation of that person by an endowment of spiritual gifts" (*Pneumatologia*, quoted in John Stott, *Baptism and Fullness*, Leicester 1975).

Older clergy were instructed at college not to have friends in the local church, since this would show favouritism. But close friendships can actually be liberating, rather than exclusive and isolationist. Jesus was never rebuked for taking aside three particular disciples, or for his special friendship with John. Ordination surely doesn't take away such basic human needs.

Someone explained to me recently the advantage of a minister owning a house in another part of the country. "You can never be yourself in the parish. You always need to be in the role of minister, even to your family when they visit." Jesus said the truth shall set you free.

We lived for a while in a town where all the ministers swapped churches one Sunday a year as an expression of Christian unity. I couldn't help but feel, at least in some cases, that it would have been a more dramatic expression of unity to stay in their own church, but to sit among the congregation, while others from the fellowship led the service. For many today, the barriers between denominations are crumbling. The frontier most sternly guarded is often between pulpit and pew.

When I was a publisher I visited many different churches. Some ministers would speak as a member of the local fellowship. Others seemed much more isolated. I admired the selflessness of so many clergy. Their sacrifices are often considerable. But the body of Christ is in peak condition when all its parts are working in harmony, not when one or two full-timers are thoroughly over-worked.

David Watson did two small things in York which had a profound impact. First, when he preached, he didn't hide from us his personal weaknesses, referring both to asthma and to bouts of depression. He would not let us put him on a pedestal. He stressed he was as frail and needy as the rest of us.

Second, he belonged to a house group, not as the leader but as a member. Some ministers say they like to visit all the groups in turn to keep an eye on them. They explain quite rightly the risks of "favouritism" if one group is adopted by them, and fear that their regular presence might inhibit the group.

It all depends on how it is organised. We visited one church in London where the minister was allocated to a group on the same geographical basis as everyone else. He didn't say too much, to avoid making others tongue-tied. Crucially, he related to the group first as "Richard", not first as "The Pastor". He was enriched and so were the other group members.

If a minister preaches that we need fellowship in house groups but then doesn't belong to one himself, his actions speak louder than words. Maybe his preaching was exaggerated, so that while home groups may suit some people, there's nothing necessary about them. Or maybe as a minister he is now above that need for fellowship the rest of us still have.

I'm not at all sure how an isolated minister, who has never learnt how to be cared for in a small group, can train group leaders to nurture that special kind of care. We have to learn to receive, in order to learn to belong.

Every member ministry doesn't make the minister redundant. On the contrary, it permits him to learn to receive from others in the body, and releases him to express his distinctive God-given gifts. Perhaps for the first time he can really become a member within the body, rather than a partially severed limb. The more the body of Christ is rediscovered, the fuller an individual ministry can be.

Over seventy years ago, an Anglican missionary to China wrote an astonishingly prophetic book, called *Missionary Methods: St Paul's or Ours?* He contrasted modern mission strategy with Paul's and concluded that imperialistic methods produce weak-kneed converts, ever dependent on European missionaries, who held all the reins and remained a priestly race apart. In the last twenty years, his words have finally struck home, not only to missionary societies, but also to patterns of Church life and ministry here in the West:

> . . . the power in which St Paul was able to act with such boldness was the Spirit of faith. Faith, not in the natural capabilities of his converts, but in the power of the Holy Ghost in them.
>
> Now if we are to practise any methods approaching to the Pauline methods in power and directness, it is absolutely necessary that we should first have this faith, this Spirit. Without faith – faith in the Holy Ghost in our converts – we can do nothing. We cannot possibly act as the Apostle acted until we recover this faith. Without it we shall be unable to recognise the grace of the Holy Spirit in our converts, we shall never trust them, we shall never inspire in them confidence in the power of the Holy Spirit in themselves. If we have no faith in the power of the Holy Spirit in them, they will not learn to have faith in the power of the Holy Spirit in themselves. We cannot trust them, and they cannot be worthy of trust; and trust, the trust which begets trustworthiness, is the one essential for any success in the Pauline method (*Missionary Methods: St Paul's or Ours?* from chapter thirteen: Application, London 1912).

Paul didn't hide his normal human weaknesses behind a mask of perfect professionalism. Some clergy suggest the gospel is best served if they conceal their own needs and limitations. Paul explained that the apostles' method was the complete opposite: "But we have this treasure in jars of clay to show that this all-surpassing power is from God and not from us" (2 Cor 4:7). We need to learn to trust the Spirit to do his work, in ministers who don't disguise they are "clay jars" as needy as any other Christian. We also need to trust the Spirit in every single Christian in our local church.

Gifts for worship

We have come a long way in considering the body of Christ and the spiritual gifts. Paul identified for the Colossians three key priorities for life together.

* As members of one body they are called to peace with God and as a result, peace with each other. Their relationships should not merely be marked by an absence of strife, but should be radiant with that peace that passes understanding (Col 3:15).
* The Word of Christ should dwell in them richly. As they teach and build up one another, together they will grow in spiritual wisdom (Col 3:16).
* Their meetings should ring with the sound of praise, in psalms, hymns and spiritual songs. Everything needs to be done in the name of Christ. As they join in constant thanks to the Father, their hearts will be filled with gratitude (Col 3:16–17).

The Corinthians were making a terrible mess of Christian living. But Jim Packer warns that this "must not blind us to the fact that they were enjoying the ministry of the Holy Spirit in a way in which we today are not" (*Keep in Step with the Spirit*, Leicester 1984).

From Paul's letters to the Corinthians we receive not only the words of institution of the Lord's Supper, but also this invaluable description of early church worship: "When you come together, everyone has a hymn, or a word of instruction, a revelation, a tongue or an interpretation" (1

Cor 14:26). Every member ministry is taken quite literally. Everyone has a gift to offer. Worship in the Spirit is characterised by rich variety. God delights in a combination of orderly preparation and spontaneous participation.

Paul's next sentence is very important: "All of these must be done for the strengthening of the church" (1 Cor 14:26). This means first that motivation must be correct. All must be done for the sake of others. If participation is based on showmanship, it cannot be of the Spirit.

At the same time, Paul stresses that for a church to be truly alive in the Spirit, its worship needs all of these elements. Hymns and instruction, prophecy and tongues, all need the freedom to be present. When all these things are done, to build each other up and not to parade our own gifts, the church is thoroughly strengthened. C. K. Barrett commented with typical English understatement: "Church meetings in Corinth can scarcely have suffered from dullness" (*Commentary on 1 Corinthians*, London 1971). I don't think Paul insists on these particular gifts at every meeting. But he does insist on the freedom to participate with a wide variety of spiritual gifts. What's more, since he says 'everyone' has something to give, this can only find practical fulfilment in many churches today through home groups.

However we apply these verses to our own fellowship, the important thing is that we don't brush them under the carpet and pretend they don't exist. We probably have to ask ourselves some uncomfortable questions: Do we pick and choose which gifts will be allowed in our church? Do we decide for ourselves who will be allowed to exercise them? Are these decisions made simply according to our personal taste in worship? If so, are we cramping the freedom of the Spirit to lead our worship and to strengthen our fellowship in the ways he desires?

There is a song some Christians could easily sing:

> If you take the gifts road,
> And I take the fruit road,
> I'm sure I'll get to heaven before you!

All who try to divide the united path of the Spirit begin to divide themselves from the one Spirit of Christ. If high altitude experience makes a Christian feel superior, his pride quenches the Spirit who blessed him. If I dismiss the experience or gifts of others out of hand, my arrogance denies the fruit I claim to desire.

The one Spirit brings assurance and holiness, wholeness and harmony in the one body of Christ. Present with us, he longs to multiply his fruit and distribute his gifts of love. Only by his Spirit can Christ renew and revive his Church.

Part Three

POPULAR EXCUSES FOR AVOIDING THE SPIRIT

9

RECEIVING THE SPIRIT

Politicians are masters of excuses. If we don't like their policies, they talk about the cure that needs a bitter pill, or say there is no alternative. Ask them a straight question, and they'll try anything rather than give a straight answer.

Any evangelism meets popular excuses. Michael Green looked at many of them in *You Must Be Joking*: Jesus was just a good man; you can't change human nature; you can't believe in God these days; and so on. Many people work hard to dodge the promise of a new beginning in Christ.

Nietzsche hit on one popular excuse to avoid Jesus: "His disciples will have to look more saved, if I am going to believe in their Saviour." Faced with such frankness, we have to confess the failure of Christians to live up to their calling, both in the past and in our own lives. But in evangelism we wouldn't stop there.

Nietzsche pointed at one thing – the Church – in order to avoid another – Jesus Christ. We would want to defuse his popular excuse by bringing him face to face with Jesus in the Gospels. No man has ever lived like Jesus. No man has ever taught like Jesus. His claims and his life make a perfect fit. He is indeed the way, the truth and the life.

I am convinced that many Christians use popular excuses to avoid the Spirit. We use slogans to try to dodge his impact on our lives, or to convince ourselves that there's nothing more for us to learn. We do this over receiving the Spirit, over life in the Spirit, and over spiritual gifts.

You may be tempted to read this part of the book first. I do hope you will read it in context. That way you might just come to it with a much fuller picture of all that the Spirit wants to do in our lives.

Excuse one: I got it all at conversion

We have seen already that only by the Spirit can anyone confess "Jesus is Lord" (1 Cor 12:3). Only by the Spirit can anyone truly believe that Jesus is God's only Son (John 4:15). Paul insists that if anyone does not have the Spirit of Christ, he does not belong to Christ (Rom 8:9), and also reveals that only by the Spirit's presence are we grafted into the body of Christ (1 Cor 12:13).

No Spirit would mean no conversion, separated from both Christ and his Church. In 1 Corinthians 12:13, Paul uses a special tense – the aorist – to stress that not only are conversion and baptism decisive moments, once-for-all, but at the same time we receive our first drink of the Spirit. The New Testament witness is unanimous: whoever receives Christ as Saviour receives his Spirit.

When children receive new presents they usually claim pride of place in the toy cupboard. Our toddler and his baby brother received one gift which causes much less excitement: special children's savings accounts. The money is theirs, and one day they'll spend it. For the moment, they have not been told about it: presents they cannot play with don't seem real presents at all.

New converts in the early Church were told all about the Spirit. They didn't just receive him in a kind of spiritual deposit account. They entered without fear or apology into the full life of the Spirit.

Our problem is not that we haven't received the Spirit. It's that, in many churches, no one is ever told anything about him, except perhaps what to avoid. It's as if someone put a large sum in the bank in our name but never told us about it.

According to the New Testament, our experience is subnormal. In the early church there was not a long gap between new birth and consciously receiving the Holy Spirit. Our problem is ignorance. "People fail to believe in the whole range of the Spirit's work, not mainly because they are defective in faith, but because the gospel that has been declared to them has been defective" (Tom Smail, *Reflected Glory*, London 1975).

When we first find out about the Spirit, fear can make things not much better. We then take this most marvellous present, given us by God, and slide it carefully under the bed for safekeeping, with its wrapping paper still on.

Such comparisons are never completely accurate. No Christian living at all is possible without the Spirit. But we treat him more like a lodger than the Lord of the Manor. We often set, from fear or ignorance, rigid boundaries to what he can do in our lives.

We are born again once only. "He who has the Son has eternal life" (John 5:12). But this once-for-all salvation is the start of a lifelong journey of discipleship. Paul encouraged the Philippians to keep pressing ahead in Christ. "Not that I have already obtained all this, or have already been made perfect, but I press on to take hold of that for which Christ Jesus took hold of me . . . to win the prize for which God has called me heavenward in Christ Jesus" (Phil 3:12–14).

It is true that we received the Spirit at conversion. It is also true that the first Christians came into an immediate experience of the Spirit's presence and power (Gal 3:2). When "got it already" starts to mean "The Spirit has nothing more to give me" or "I don't want any more of the Spirit", a biblical truth has been distorted into a popular excuse. What we begin to mean is "got it all", and that just doesn't make sense. Martin Lloyd-Jones would have none of this excuse for avoiding the Spirit:

Got it all? Well, if you have "got it all" I simply ask, in the name of God, why are you as you are? If you have got it all, why are you so unlike the New Testament Christians? Got it all? Got it all at your conversion? Well, where is it I ask? (*Westminster Record*, Sep 1964).

Excuse two: Talk about the Holy Spirit distracts from Christ

A child with a brand new toy can talk of nothing else. Infatuated teenage lovers only have eyes for each other. In the same way, some Christians are so thrilled to rediscover the Spirit that they seem unable to talk of anything else. A few even suggest that you graduate from life in Christ to life in the Spirit.

It is not like that in the New Testament. Only through the cross is the Spirit given. The Spirit has a floodlight ministry, always highlighting the Son and the Father. It is the Spirit who equips the Church, but we become part of the Body of Christ, not the body of the Spirit. The Spirit delights to bring glory to Christ.

This doesn't mean that Christ is best glorified by never mentioning the Spirit. He is the Spirit of Jesus, sent from the Father and the Son. When we talk about the Spirit biblically, it is Jesus who is glorified.

Jesus and the apostles saw that detailed and direct teaching about the Spirit is vital. During Jesus' last week before the crucifixion, he by no means only talked about the Spirit. But John's gospel reveals that the promise of the Spirit was one of the central themes of Jesus' final teaching.

You cannot exchange Jesus for the Spirit. Talking exclusively about the Spirit does distract from Christ. But passing over the Spirit in silence or cautious whispers plays down all that Jesus has provided for us.

Glorifying Christ is no excuse for avoiding the Spirit. The more we are truly open to the Spirit, the more Christ can be glorified, both on our lips and in our lives.

Excuse three: Talk about being filled with the Spirit creates second class Christians

If this were true, the apostle Paul would be at fault. He nowhere tells established Christians to be "baptised in the Spirit", as a post-conversion experience. But he certainly urges born-again Christians to be filled. Paul's desire for the Ephesians and God's intention for his Church is that every Christian should be filled with the Spirit. "Do not get drunk on wine, which leads to debauchery. Instead be filled with the Spirit" (Eph 5:18).

This is not an optional extra for the enthusiastic. All Christians need to be filled with the Spirit. Nor is this one possible sideshow for livening up discipleship. To be filled with the Spirit isn't a suggestion, it is an invitation and a command.

Paul is very careful to use the present continuous tense. Just as we are born again, once-for-all, he could have written: be filled once-for-all. Instead he wrote: go on being filled. A successful blood transfusion refills the system, which can then look after itself. No more outside help is needed. Living in the Spirit is more like the petrol tank on a car with an outsize engine – in constant need of refilling.

When we talk about the "fullness of the Spirit" it can sound like a point of arrival. It may suggest that once we are filled, we are permanently filled. In the light of Paul's careful choice of words, we need to reject that impression.

Moody's comment on being filled with the Spirit is still helpful. He said he had been filled, but he leaked. Sin quenches the Spirit. As we minister to others the Spirit flows out from us. When we are tired or overworked, we can become more remote from God. It's quite possible to stop being filled with the Spirit because in all these different ways we "leak". Jesus spoke of the Spirit as "rivers of living water" precisely because we need him continually to keep on flowing through our lives.

The Spirit is far more than "spiritual petrol". Ezekiel once described Israel as an old cooking pot, on which burnt food and rust had gradually encrusted (Ezek 24). That blackened encrusting represented the sin which disfigured Israel. As the Spirit works within us, he wants increasingly to scour the refuse out of our lives, and set us free, shining like new, as the people God made us to be. The more the

Spirit works, the more inner space he creates. As he fills us, he creates the possibility of filling us even more.

Commitment has been described as giving all you know of yourself to all you know of God. As the Spirit leads us into all truth, he reveals more of ourselves, in need of surrendering to God, and more of God, and his inexhaustible love for each of his children. As the Spirit enlarges our self-awareness and our discovery of God, he continually deepens what it can mean to be filled with him. Above all, the Spirit turns upside down our natural desire to be in control of our relationship with God: "If you think of him only as an influence, you will be anxious that you may have more of it; but if you think of him as a person, you will desire that he may have more of you" (Torrey).

Paul contrasts being filled with the Spirit to getting drunk. The drunk is no help to anyone else: the Spirit prompts and pushes us beyond the limits of self-interest. When someone is drunk, others suffer: when someone is filled with the Spirit, others benefit.

A third contrast is often added: while a drunk loses control of himself, one of the marks of the Spirit is self-discipline (2 Tim 1:7). We need to see that Paul's contrast is by no means between normal respectability and drunkenness. Of course the Spirit brings a new kind of self control. True spirituality is not marked above all else, either in Jesus or in the early church, by some kind of ecstatic frenzy. But spiritual self control is not always the same as super-respectability.

We say that a drunk is "under the influence" of alcohol. At Pentecost the Christians were "under the influence" of the Spirit. The Spirit had taken unmistakable control of their lives. The New Testament never suggests the apostles seemed permanently drunk to outsiders, but they certainly did on this occasion. What's more, being filled with the Spirit wasn't the special privilege of "spiritual superstars". It continues to be the calling of every single Christian, every single day.

We need to feel slightly disturbed by Paul's careful

comparison. This isn't a rather grand and religious way of saying "Don't drink too much." Paul is not merely recommending respectable sobriety. He is urging Christians to surrender control, not to alcohol but to the Spirit.

We saw that at conversion we receive our first drink of the Spirit. Those rivers of living water never run dry. One sip is not meant to last a lifetime. The Spirit doesn't want to be an occasional Christian tipple. He doesn't want to top up our lives from time to time. He wants to immerse us in himself. And he wants day by day control.

Sometimes Christians lose their thirst for God. They begin to act as if they can cope quite well without outside help. This is disastrous. I remember David Watson speaking of many ministers and missionaries coming to see him to confess a terrible spiritual dryness. They lacked an inner sense of the presence and power of God, both for effective change in their own lives and for effective ministry to others.

Where Christians are not being filled with the Spirit, there is a terrible blight on the church. John Stott has warned that the "dead, dry bones of the Church need the living breath of God" (*Baptism and Fullness*, Leicester 1975). Jim Packer is even more frank about our spiritual desert: ". . . we inherit today a situation in which the Spirit of God has been quenched. Unnatural as it may be, the Spirit's power is absent from the majority of our churches" (*Keep in Step with the Spirit*, Leicester 1984).

Israel faced a similar problem. The Hebrews had to stop living in the past. They had to open their minds and their hearts to God's new activity:

> Forget the former things;
> do not dwell on the past.
> See I am doing a new thing!
> Now it springs up; do you not perceive it?
> I am making a way in the desert
> and streams in the wasteland.
>
> (Isa 43:18–19)

It wasn't that God was contradicting himself. He never does that. But if you live in the past, you exchange a living faith for a dead orthodoxy. You still hold to the outward form of religion, but you have lost its inner power.

Two verses before Paul stressed the very first drink of the Spirit by each new Christian, he described the Spirit *"energising"* the Church (1 Cor 12:11). This isn't like the single electric shock which set Frankenstein in motion. The Spirit is the heart and the lifeblood of the Church. He is always at work, moment by moment and generation by generation, always wanting us to receive something more from God.

Gavin Reid, the National Director of Mission England, summed up the vast gap between our typical church life and the constantly re-energised churches of the first century: "The plain fact of the matter is that even the best evangelical religion bears little resemblance to the experience of the Apostles. We have conditioned ourselves not to notice this . . ." (*Church of England Newspaper*).

So how do we get from our ignorance to the apostolic experience? That's where the problems begin. Everyone is agreed that our spiritual condition is pretty poor, but many get hot under the collar the moment we try to bridge the gap. Talk about the Spirit is quickly understood to be "pulling rank" on other Christians, by claiming a second stage experience.

We need to see how this has come about, but first we need to see that the whole difficulty arises from our inadequate teaching about the Spirit:

* The New Testament reveals I received the Spirit at conversion. But when I was converted, nobody told me anything about him.
* The New Testament tells us to go on being filled with the Spirit. But many of us were encouraged to be suspicious, or quickly change the subject, if anyone started talking about the Spirit. We were scared to

know any more about him in theory, let alone in practice.

* The New Testament doesn't say to Christians that we should *start* being filled. The New Testament writers take it for granted that converts receive proper teaching. For them, being filled with the Spirit doesn't start at some later experience, it is part of becoming a Christian. Being filled with the Spirit was as much part of Christian initiation as baptism.

Our ignorance cannot prevent us receiving the Spirit in the first place. But to say that we are continually being immersed in the life-transforming power of the Spirit, even without actually knowing about it, does seem to stretch the evidence a great deal.

Paul wanted no Christian to settle for second best. But it's very difficult to hold together on the one hand the promise of inner change and on the other the warning that final perfection cannot be achieved in this life. John Wesley wanted to recover Paul's vision of inner renewal. He always stressed he hadn't arrived himself. Yet in his concern to counteract half-heartedness, he certainly seemed to suggest you could ascend to a plateau of perfection.

Paul said holiness was hard work, but in the power of the Spirit it could be a pathway of gradual improvement. Half-hearted Christians had come to say that any real holiness this side of the grave was an impossible dream. For some of Wesley's followers, holiness became a definite destination. Gradual improvement turned into an achievement of perfection. Once you arrived, there was no going back. Your problems were over.

Out of the Wesleyans grew the nineteenth century holiness movements. The central concern was never to invent a new Christian elite. All they wanted was to reclaim the New Testament vision of spiritual renewal in this life. After all, the first Christians were recognisable not only by their beliefs, but by the unmistakable quality of their lives.

The problem wasn't the desire for holiness. Of course not. Nor was it dramatic experience. Many Christians in every age have experienced moments of sudden spiritual growth. The problem was the tendency to see Christian living like a two-storey building. Once you had a certain kind of experience, or a period of marked inner progress, it was understood you had ascended to the upper floor.

I think Paul would welcome the desire for holiness, praise God for the experience, but question the explanation. According to his teaching, if you want to see holiness as a building, it's not a two-storey home but a high-rise with far too many floors to count. That shouldn't frustrate us. It simply means there's always more that God can do in our lives.

Two-storey thinking didn't just confuse how you understood an experience. It could also make you feel quite literally "one up" on other Christians. If you did feel superior, that would seem to contradict any claim to advanced holiness. But feelings of false superiority were almost inevitable, until people turned back from the two-storey house to the high-rise.

It's like walking in a mountain range. A crag looms above you, dominating the skyline. You are sure it must be the highest point as you clamber up. As you get nearer the top, the view below is stunning. Only as you reach the very peak do you realise that an even higher crag lies further ahead, obscured until now by the one just climbed. In this life, God has never finished with you. His blessings are never exhausted. No Christian has ever arrived.

Two-storey thinking also created a "throwing out the baby with the bathwater" problem. The theology might not have been precisely biblical, but the holiness movement earnestly desired to rekindle the first Christians' passion for inner renewal. Some who didn't accept the perfection of the upper floor, ended up missing out on the renewed quest for holiness at the same time.

The same has happened this century with the Spirit. The first Pentecostals had to look around for some kind of explanation for their dramatic new experience. They were in circles influenced by the holiness movement, and so they adopted very similar two stage thinking. The second stage was the baptism in the Spirit, automatically accompanied by tongues.

In the last twenty five years, many hundreds of thousands of Christians have started rediscovering the Spirit. Many exercise personally the gift of tongues, but do not suggest that it is the particular or necessary sign of the Spirit. Many do not hold to two-storey thinking, and do not teach a second stage baptism. Instead, they encourage a new openness to keep on being filled with the Spirit. They desire that every Christian may be set free in the way that has been possible ever since the Spirit was first poured out on the Church.

I remember one flourishing evangelical church where God was doing a great deal. But there was a real blockage concerning the Spirit. Every so often, the minister would give a talk warning against the charismatic movement. Instead of looking at biblical teaching on the Spirit, he concentrated on the history of the holiness movement, and where it had "gone wrong". That, he explained, was the root of the mistakes of the charismatics, who were simply the old holiness movement with new jargon.

There were three big problems. First the Holy Spirit seemed neatly disposed of at the same time as the two-storey thinking. It was as if the congregation needn't worry about the Spirit any more. He was received at conversion, and that was the end of that.

Second, in rejecting two-stage teaching, he seemed to dismiss any post-conversion experience of the Spirit. Experience can be genuine even when the explanation isn't quite right. One New Testament scholar caused a stir about ten years ago by saying that although he didn't think Pentecostal theology was accurately biblical, Pentecostal *experience* of the Spirit was much closer to the early church than that of most conventional Christians.

Of course, there are some Christians who claim superior

status *for themselves*, through their particular experience of the Spirit. This should hardly be surprising. Christian groups have, after all, claimed superiority for themselves through just about everything else: brand of liturgy, style of Lord's Supper, quantity of baptismal water, fashions of clerical clothing, hymn book, architecture and preferred Bible translation. Of course, if only those with a strictly Pentecostal experience are on the upper floor, then the second class Christians include not only Calvin and Luther, but also Billy Graham and Mother Theresa!

The third and even more decisive problem with this excuse is, quite simply, that many "charismatics" do *not* teach that experience of the Spirit is on two floors only. This is true for example of both Michael Green and Michael Cassidy, and was also true of David Watson.

Anyone who reduces discussion of being filled with the Spirit to what is wrong with two-stage thinking is using a popular excuse to avoid the Spirit. Don't try to dodge the need to go on being filled. Don't try to use someone else's mistakes as a red herring.

Leaving aside two-storey thinking, that still leaves us the problem of how to bridge the gap from sub-standard teaching and experience to being filled with the Spirit. I used to commute to London. Imagine if someone bought me as a Christmas present an annual British Rail season ticket. If they forgot to tell me about it until July, free journeys would have been available to me for six months, while I had still been paying for tickets day by day.

Nothing could make up for the lost money. But I wouldn't waste any more. The ticket inspector would doubtless examine the season ticket very carefully the next day. You aren't allowed to use someone else's, and it is not exactly usual to start using an expensive annual season ticket half way through the year.

You have to start somewhere. It would be better to start using the ticket in July than never use it at all. Abnormal circumstances require unusual action. It's very similar with the Holy Spirit.

There is no strict need, in the New Testament, for any crisis moment after conversion when you begin to ask to be filled. Being filled can be part of your Christian life from the beginning. But if you've gone through three months or thirty years without consciously asking to be filled, you've got to start somewhere. And it would be far better to start now than not at all.

Starting to be filled doesn't make you a superior Christian. It simply means that you are starting to live out in practice what has been available to you ever since your very first drink of the Spirit. Being filled with the Spirit doesn't create first and second class Christians. It simply means obeying the God of grace, and not turning away from his Holy Spirit after the very first sip.

10

IN STEP WITH THE SPIRIT

I want to look now at the four most popular excuses which point the finger at some charismatics. I don't want to pretend such problems don't exist, but it is foolish to reject the Spirit of God because of someone else's mistakes.

Excuse one: It's all crisis geared

If you asked round your church how people were converted you'd discover many different stories. Many would be able to put a definite date on their conversion. Many others would struggle even to identify a definite month. At a certain point they were not yet committed. Later, they knew they believed. But in between there is a very blurred period, where it is hard to make out any clear pattern.

That doesn't mean evangelists are wrong to stress the need for a definite commitment. Some respond there and then. Others are prompted to think about it. For others it can set a public seal on a conviction which has been growing in them for a long time.

The only time an evangelist would be mistaken would be if he insisted that only one particular kind of conversion experience was genuine, and tried to press-gang every individual into the same mould. We are all very different. We make our responses to Christ in very different ways. It is as unique individuals that the Spirit is at work in each of us.

It is just the same with Christian growth. Most of us can look back to periods of very gradual progress, and also to moments when we made a sudden spurt, like trees in spring that burst into full leaf almost over night. Perhaps, like me, you can also look back and see other periods of gradual but unmistakable decline: it's no good banking on last season's fruit, for God wants you to be growing today.

We need to appreciate the value of variety. There is no single blueprint for Christian growth. But just as with evangelism, we need to recognise that, for many people, there will be a decisive breakthrough, when they finally escape from ignorance or fear of the Spirit. That won't be the end of their rediscovery of the Spirit. It will be more like a beginning.

In this context I want, very briefly, to describe a breakthrough experience of my own. Like a testimony of conversion, this isn't the only way God works, but it is the way he dealt with a particular person. For me, this was a crucial experience which bridged the gap between a deficient or substandard modern conversion, and the biblical freedom to go on being filled with the Spirit.

It was mid spring 1976. The evening service at St. Michael-le-Belfrey, York, was a communion. That always meant a very special time of worship, "lost in wonder, love and praise".

Suddenly David Watson suggested something new. After everyone had received the bread and wine, there would be an opportunity to come forward for prayer for special needs.

My heart warmed within me. It wasn't that I had any particular need myself. But I had been used to rather traditional communion services: you queued in silence waiting for a space at the rail; you received the bread and wine through formal words without any personal addition; and then you returned to your pew, carefully avoiding eye contact with any other worshipper. It felt so much more in harmony with the New Testament vision of the Church to have this time of personal encouragement and ministry.

As the singing group led us in quiet and sensitive worship, the first two or three went forward for prayer. It was only then that I experienced an overwhelming sense that God wanted me to go forward. I'd never felt anything quite like it before. It was as if someone had just switched on a powerful electric magnet in my stomach. But I distrusted emotions. So I stayed firmly sitting in my pew.

A few minutes later the feeling returned. I still didn't know for what particular need I was meant to go forward. Again I pushed the feeling away and sat tight.

The time of ministry was just about over. No one else seemed to be going forward. Then the powerful magnetic pull started up a third time.

I had started the service feeling absolutely fine. Now I knew of a deep need within. I had resisted the prompting twice, but I knew I could ignore it no longer. If I resisted any more, I would return to my college room acutely aware of an unmet need. I simply had to go forward.

As I approached the altar rail where the elders were ministering, my need came into sharp focus. I knew I had received the Spirit at conversion. But now I realised I had been holding back from him. I realised too how little love I had for others, compared with the love of Christ. With a faltering voice I asked that God might fill me more with his Spirit and give me more of his love for others.

I knelt down and hands were gently laid on my head. The elder thanked God for his promises about the Spirit and claimed them for me. As he prayed, I opened my heart and life to God deeper than I had ever dared or dreamed before. Then the prayer showed great wisdom. The request turned into thanks. Just as at conversion we can thank God that now we are saved, the elder thanked God that now he was indeed filling me in a new way, just as he had promised.

One friend told me afterwards that when I stood up to go forward I looked absolutely dreadful – more grim than she had ever seen me. On the way back my face shone with a joy never seen there before. I was radiant with the Spirit of God.

That wasn't the end of my problems as a Christian. By no means! But it was an absolutely crucial moment of release. I lay in bed that night aglow in the Spirit. God was present to me in a way I had never known before. The indwelling of the Spirit was now a living reality, and not just an item of doctrine.

For several hours I stayed awake, to praise God and to bask in this glorious immersion in the Spirit. You may think me very foolish when I tell you that, as I lay there, I wiggled my toes and with tears of joy I cried out, "You are even there, right down in my toes!"

I don't tell you my story to suggest that this is a blueprint experience for each and every Christian. That would be nonsense. I simply tell you because, perhaps for you as well as for me, the way to begin to go-on-being-filled is through a decisive moment of new openness.

This doesn't mean you ascend to a compulsory second floor where your spiritual status goes up a notch. Far from it. But God does want you to begin to enter fully into the glorious promises of the Spirit. The Holy Spirit does indeed want to keep on changing you, even in this life. He longs to transform us more and more into Christ's likeness by his presence within. "And we . . . are being transformed into his [Christ's] likeness with ever-increasing glory, which comes from the Lord, who is the Spirit" (2 Cor 3:18).

Excuse two: It's all emotions

When Peter and John healed the man at the Beautiful Gate, he caused quite a stir. After all those terrible years of begging, his legs had been made whole. He didn't just walk into the temple to thank God, he skipped and leaped his way round those hallowed precincts. He was jumping for joy (Acts 3:1–10).

I'm sure some of the temple priests weren't at all pleased. You can imagine their snide criticism: "That's what happens if you mix with the followers of Jesus – you lose all sense of respect for the house of God!"

There's no suggestion that the healed man praised God by leaping about for the rest of his life. Perhaps he never again quite literally jumped for joy. But I'm sure his heart leaped within him, whenever he remembered in worship all that God had done that day.

British people find it notoriously hard to express emotion. When we are so far out of touch with our own feelings, any emotional display in public is likely to make us uncomfortable. We are quick to label almost anything as over-emotional. When a publisher wants a picture of a happy crowd, he turns last of all to photos of the British: no matter how happy some look, a significant minority will probably look bored or glum.

We are like pressure cookers, locking away our pent-up emotions deep inside. We desperately need the pressure released. But if the lid comes off too quickly, there's almost bound to be an explosion.

I remember hearing two very different sermons on emotions. An Anglican vicar warned his parishioners about the dangers of excessive emotion. The gospel can be reduced to froth and bubbles and to "getting a good feeling". Then a Pentecostal pastor cautioned his flock about the desert of an emotion-free gospel. New life in Christ can be withered away into no more than dry-as-dust theory.

Both were right. But how I wish they had been preaching from each other's pulpits. We see other people's over-emphasis so much more clearly than our own!

The word normally used for worship in the New Testament originally meant "I come towards to kiss." That is the kind of intimacy we need to rediscover in worship. Courting couples don't often discuss at great depth the psychology of interpersonal behaviour. They usually find more value in saying and saying again those time-honoured words: "I love you." There is always a need for thoughtful hymns, expressing in great poetry all that we have been given in Christ. But there is also room for simple love songs to be sung by the bride of Christ.

I wonder what some Christians would make of the worship of Ancient Israel. There were exciting psalms which relived the events of the deliverance from Egypt. There were meditative psalms on the glories of God's law.

And there were enthusiastic psalms which praised God with very simple words and a great deal of repetition.

Some psalms allowed God's people to tell him just how terrible they felt. They could even complain to God that they felt hard done by. This type was linked to temple prophecy: you could get your bad feelings off your chest, but then you had to wait, humbly and quietly, for God's response.

The accompaniment was as varied as the words. Many different kinds of string instruments were played, along with pipes, drums and cymbals. Psalm 150 needed a large Hebrew orchestra:

"Praise him with the sounding of the trumpet,
    praise him with the harp and lyre,
Praise him with tambourine and dancing,
    praise him with the strings and flute,
Praise him with the clash of cymbals,
    praise him with resounding cymbals.

Let everything that has breath praise the LORD."
(Psa 150:3–6)

There was also a great deal of movement. For some psalms there was a dramatic singing procession, marching round the temple or even around the city. They clapped their hands, stood up in God's presence, and raised their hands before him.

Then there was the festal shout. At special celebrations the cry went up from the people: "The Lord reigns!" This great shout of praise and triumph would make the temple ring. Yahweh is Lord above all lords. No one can take his place or overturn his plans. As they celebrated Yahweh the King, the people renewed their homage and obedience to him.

Temple worship also included dancing. You may have noticed it in Psalm 150, tucked in between the tambourine and the strings. That is by no means the only reference. In Psalm 87, singers and dancers alike praise God the source of their vitality (v 7). And in Psalm 149 the whole of Israel is called to worship which includes dance:

> Let Israel rejoice in their Maker;
>> let the people of Zion be glad in their King,
> Let them praise his name with dancing
>> and make music to him with tambourine and harp
>>>> (Psa 149:2–3).

Jeremiah delighted in this glorious experience of worshipping God with all that we are. When he prophesied the new covenant in chapter thirty-one, he saw that in the coming age, worship could be even richer and joy even more full. He foretold that the worship of the new covenant would find a special place for dance:

> They will come and shout for joy on the heights of Zion;
>> they will rejoice in the bounty of the LORD . . .
> . . . Then maidens will dance and be glad,
>> young men and old as well.
> I will turn their mourning into gladness;
>> I will give them comfort and joy instead of sorrow
>>>> (Jer 31:12–13).

Because God made us, all that we are, bodies and emotions as well as minds and voices, can be put to good use in worship. We are constantly using non-verbal communication in the way we sit and move. Many use gestures to reinforce what they say. Italians are so good at it that I have followed a complete conversation without understanding more than a handful of the spoken words. There really is no biblical reason why we should only be allowed to sing hymns while standing to attention.

Fear of emotions can make us very emotional. We run scared from a healthy wholeness in worship. All kinds of horrors have been read into styles of worship that the ancient Israelites would have considered perfectly normal.

Jesus wept in public before Lazarus' tomb: emotions are

given for appropriate expression, not to be hidden away guiltily, far from public view. Paul told us to learn to weep with those who weep, and rejoice with those who rejoice. He didn't expect us to repress all our feelings so that we never rock the respectable boat of formal public worship.

Rediscovering emotions takes the lid off the pressure cooker. For a while we can be so entranced by emotions that we go over the top. I remember one fellowship for whom Sunday evening was a regular emotional high. Then they gradually sank back into gloom through the week until their emotions were stoked back up again. If you didn't fit in with their weekly emotional cycle, then you couldn't fit in at all.

Emotions are one part of us to be expressed in worship. Emotions are not the focus or purpose of worship. I have to confess that at times I have come to worship not first because God is worthy of all praise, but because I wanted a good feeling from worship.

True worship may well lift your feelings. But if you look to feelings instead of to God, true worship will begin to shrivel. Before long your emotions will become dry, bland and stale.

The Spirit never gives us emotion for emotion's sake. But always remember the prophecy of Jeremiah about exuberant rejoicing in the new covenant. Remember too that one of Luke's favourite phrases for being filled with the Spirit is that Christians became "*filled with great joy*".

Excuse three: It's all triumphalism

Triumphalism means disguising discipleship as a never-failing success story. It means glamorising the gospel as a failsafe way to find spiritual thrills.

Triumphalism isn't based on service of God. It is rooted in self-fulfilment: "What's in it for me?" It holds out the spiritualised equivalent of advertising slogans, and plays down the demands of the gospel and the problems of everyday living.

The Philippians were probably Paul's favourite church.
They had a lot going for them, and didn't suffer from the
turmoil and confusion Paul had to sort out in some cities.
Then the trouble started. The other citizens of Philippi
began to oppose the Christians (Phil 1:28).

Cracks opened up in the fellowship. Some grabbed status
for themselves. Some concentrated only on their own
"in-crowd". Some settled into constant complaints and
arguments. Their question for Paul was simple: "Why is
King Jesus letting us be treated like this?"

Paul wrote to them from prison. He had been imprisoned
before – in Philippi itself, of all places. Acts 16 records how
the Spirit miraculously freed him. Luke rejoices that the
Spirit's power can set prisoners free, just as Isaiah had
prophesied. But the story doesn't stop there.

The last seven chapters of the book of Acts – one quarter
of its total length – are devoted to Paul's long imprisonment. This time there is no sudden deliverance. The Spirit
never guarantees that particular solution to persecution. This time God's interests were served best by Paul
being taken to Rome, the Empire's capital, under military
escort.

If we want to recover the great triumphs known by the
early church in the power of the Spirit, we also have to be
prepared to follow them in the way of the cross. The Spirit
of Jesus is the Spirit of deliverance; but he is also the Spirit
of the martyrs.

Paul wants the Philippians to rejoice, faced both with his
imprisonment and with their own persecution. The Spirit
doesn't keep us clear of every difficulty but he helps us to
praise God through them.

More than that, Paul reveals that the Spirit wants the
Philippians to see their suffering as a privilege, and not just
a problem: "For it has been granted you on behalf of Christ
not only to believe on him, but also to suffer for him" (Phil
1:29).

This is not said lightly. No one should ever say this
casually or flippantly to someone who is suffering. Paul

writes with authority because at that very moment he himself is suffering for Christ.

Life in the Spirit doesn't mean brushing our problems under the carpet and pretending they don't exist. The Spirit helps us to accept the hard times, to trust that God will use them for good, and to rejoice in Christ, even when it hurts. That's not always easy, but it's in a different league to artificial glamour and soap-sud slogans.

Excuse four: Talk about the Holy Spirit is divisive

The Holy Spirit is given to unite us. We often use him as an excuse for our divisions. The Holy Spirit points to Jesus. We often try to use him to point out what's wrong with the "other side".

The Spirit of God *never* causes splits. That must be said immediately. When Christians divide from each other, it brings great sadness and pain to the one Spirit of the one Body of Christ. Perhaps nothing quenches the Spirit more than when we reject a fellow Christian.

The Spirit gets blamed for splits because we are so keen on developing an "us and them" mentality. We claim the exclusive presence of the Spirit for our particular group. Pride and party spirit consume all sense of proportion, so we grow blind to our own faults. Whether we are too proud of the old ways or too proud of a new experience, we act as if no one has anything to teach us about the Spirit.

A second century Christian contrasted helpfully the Spirit of God and the spirit of division:

. . . the man who has the Spirit from above is filled with gentleness, patience and calm. He knows himself to be small and abstains from all wickedness and from the vain desires of this world-age. He makes himself poorer than all other men . . . The man who only imagines that he has the Spirit exalts himself. He wants to have the place of honour, and he straightaway becomes impudent,

shameless and talkative, given to excessive eating and
drinking and well versed in all kinds of trickery . . .
(*Shepherd of Hermas*)

We urgently need to recognise that there are both gains
and losses in almost every style of Christian worship. The
body of Christ extends beyond our personal prejudices and
the barriers at denominational boundaries. When we try to
dismember the body by "unchurching" our brothers and
sisters, we are all the losers. There is sometimes a painful
truth in this parody of "Onward Christian Soldiers":

Like a mighty tortoise moves the Church of God
    Brothers we are treading where we've always trod.
We are all divided, many bodies we,
    Very strong on doctrine, weak on charity.

It is simply tragic when someone says: "If that's what
happens when you go charismatic, I want nothing more to
do with the Spirit!"

One elderly lady told me about the modern songs in her
church. They were too fast, too new and too often! She felt
badly left out, and seemed to have some cause for griev-
ance. Her generation didn't feel they mattered any more.
She blamed it all on the church "going charismatic". She
was hurt by the immaturity of some young enthusiasts, but
risked hitting back by rejecting the Spirit altogether.

I remember one minister comparing his denomination
with all the rest: "You worship God in your ways and
we'll worship him in his!" Behind the intended humour I
suspected a deep and divisive arrogance.

By the one Spirit we were all baptised into the one body.
He is the Spirit of forgiveness and fellowship, not of endless
new divisions. Only by the Holy Spirit can the undivided
body of Christ be seen as a living reality, both within the
local church and beyond it.

Where a split has sadly already taken place, there is
surely one thing that has to be done. Far from going in for

187

recriminations against "the other lot", and far even from ignoring their continued existence, I am sure the Spirit would have us regularly pray God's blessing upon them. Where the Spirit is, there is hope of renewal *and* reconciliation.

11

THE GIFTS OF THE SPIRIT

Excuse one: They died with the apostles

If the gifts died with the apostles, their absence from many churches today is not a problem. The common suggestion is that the apostles needed certain gifts to launch the church. Once the apostolic foundation had been laid, and the books of the New Testament had been written, certain spiritual gifts became redundant and simply ceased. There is only one problem with this description. It didn't happen that way.

We saw in chapter eight that it takes a lot of ingenuity to read into 1 Corinthians chapter thirteen the idea that the gifts died with the apostles. If you are convinced of that already, you can read it into the text. But it would have been very hard indeed for the Corinthians to take this meaning from what Paul actually wrote.

What's more, when Paul lists the necessary elements for regular worship in the next chapter (1 Cor 14:26), prophecy and tongues are mixed in with preaching and hymns. If Paul really had known that the spiritual gifts were only for his generation, it seems most extraordinary that he didn't give more help to plan ahead. At the very least he would surely have numbered the short-term gifts in a separate list, and explained the adjustments needed to public worship once they passed out of use.

Paul sums up by urging the Corinthians not to forbid speaking in tongues, and then – still worse in the eyes of some anti-charismatics – actually encourages them all to be "eager to prophesy" (1 Cor 14:39). Paul doesn't lay plans for the days without the gifts. Instead he positively encourages the gifts to flourish.

Did the gifts cease at the end of the apostolic age? It would have been a remarkable miracle. Just imagine the correspondence between the churches. Gradually they discover that in every fellowship there were no more prophecies, no more healings, and no more tongues on exactly the same day. Someone keeps on checking and, sure enough, on that very day the last surviving apostle died.

Suddenly everything makes sense. Just as the apostles had taught, when the last apostle died he took the spiritual gifts with him. We would surely expect some reference in that generation's sermons or letters to this overnight change in the worship of the Church. But of such evidence there is no trace.

Either the gifts died with the apostles or they didn't. This is not an issue for half measures. If the gifts didn't evaporate overnight, we need a less reassuring explanation for their general absence today.

The evidence from the early generations isn't of one or two unusual incidents. Nor are the witnesses to spiritual gifts unreliable or scoundrels. The most respected leaders from the mid-second century to the early third century speak with one voice. They lived close to the age of the apostles, and would surely remember any decisive moment when the gifts stopped. Instead, they testify that the Spirit is still active in the Church, and he is still bestowing his gifts.

Justin Martyr was a leading Christian at Rome. He was executed in AD 165 for refusing to sacrifice to pagan gods. In an evangelistic book he described spiritual gifts: "Even to this day the gifts of prophecy are alive among us: you can see among us both men and women who are endowed with gifts of grace" (*Dialogue with Trypho* 82).

Eusebius, the famous church historian of the fourth century, quoted Irenaeus, Bishop of Lyons, who died some time after AD 180. Irenaeus cites the spiritual gifts in the church as evidence that Jesus really worked miracles, rather than conjuring tricks:

Some drive out demons really and truly, so that often those cleansed from evil spirits believe and become members of the Church; some have foreknowledge of the future, visions and prophetic utterances; others, by the laying on of hands, heal the sick and restore them to health; and before now, as I said, dead men have actually been raised and have remained with us for many years . . . Similarly, we hear of many members of the Church who have prophetic gifts and by the Spirit speak with all kinds of tongues, and bring men's secret thoughts to light for their own good, and expound the mysteries of God (Eusebius *History of the Church* 5:7 trans G. A. Williamson, London 1965).

Irenaeus stressed that the complete range of gifts was still available to the Church and could be found in regular use: "In fact, it is impossible to enumerate the gifts which throughout the world the Church has received from God . . . freely she received from God, and freely she ministers" (Eusebius 5:7).

Faced with such evidence, Eusebius concluded: "This will suffice to show that diversity of gifts continued among fit persons till the time I am speaking of" (Eusebius 5:7).

In the mid-second century, a number of Church leaders were considered prophets, including Hermas, Polycarp and Melito. Hermas explained how to discern true prophecy and encouraged Christians to "trust the Spirit who comes from God and has power, but do not believe the earthly, empty spirit at all." (*Shepherd of Hermas*).

We still have a copy of one sermon preached by Melito, Bishop of Sardis, in which at one moment he is preaching in his usual style, then suddenly the tone is transformed. Christ begins to speak through him in words of prophecy:

Who will contend against me? Let him stand before me.
It is I who delivered the condemned. It is I who gave life to the dead.
It is I who raised up the buried. Who will argue with me?

It is I, says Christ, who destroyed death. It is I who
triumphed over the enemy,
And trod down Hades, and bound the Strong Man,
And snatched mankind up to the heights of heaven. It is
I, says Christ.
So then, come here all you families of men, weighed
down by your sins
And receive pardon for your misdeeds. For I am your
pardon.
I am the Passover which brings salvation. I am your life,
your resurrection.
I am your light, I am your salvation, I am your King.
It is I who brings you up to the heights of heaven.
It is I who will give you the resurrection there.
I will show you the Eternal Father. I will raise you up
with my own right hand.

(*Homily on the Pascha* Papyrus Bodmer 13.
quoted in Michael Green, *Evangelism in the Early
Church*, London 1970)

Tertullian (c. 160–215) eventually gave up on the established Church and joined a fanatical breakaway group
which finally fizzled out. But long before he joined the
Montanists he wrote very positively about the continued
value and use of spiritual gifts. He said it was the bishops,
not the Spirit of God, who had taken the gifts away from
the Church, by trying to keep all the gifts to themselves. A
few years later, Origen (185–254) reported that he had
witnessed in "mainline" churches healings, prophecies and
the casting out of evil spirits.

The Montanists were the final nail in the coffin of freedom for spiritual gifts. Some of their prophets started to
claim that only they possessed the Spirit. They tried to
substitute their latest prophecies for the New Testament
revelation, and even decreed where and when the second
coming would happen.

The response of the official Church was to control the
laity more than ever, and focus the spiritual gifts more and

more in the hands of the priests. In time only ordained men could preach, and then only ordained men could prophesy. Gradually the distinctive gift of prophecy dropped out of public use.

Not everyone agreed with this policy. As late as the fourth century Cyril, Bishop of Jerusalem, still thought it possible for those being baptised to receive the gift of prophecy. But he didn't rock the boat too much by stressing that he thought it wasn't very likely in practice!

More typical of the fourth century was John Chrysostom, who took it for granted that the gifts had passed through a terminal decline. He considered they were no longer given to the Church. Augustine thought the same as a young Christian, and dismissed the possibility of healing miracles in his own generation. Later, he discovered and recorded just how much God was still doing:

> For when I saw, in our own times, frequent signs of the presence of divine powers similar to those which had been given of old, I desired that narratives might be written, judging that the multitude should not remain ignorant of these things. It is not yet two years since [we began the list] . . . and though many of the miracles which have been wrought have not, as I have the most certain means of knowing, been recorded, those which have been published amount almost to seventy at the hour at which I write (*City of God* 22:8:21 trans. M. Dods, New York 1948).

Through the first four centuries we see a gradual decline of spiritual vitality. The more respectable the Church became, and the more ordained men claimed exclusive control of Christian ministry, the less the spiritual gifts were desired and given. John Wesley summed up this sad story:

> The grand reason why the miraculous gifts were so soon withdrawn was not only that faith and holiness were well-nigh lost, but that dry, formal, orthodox men began

even then to ridicule whatever gifts they had not themselves; and to decry them all, as either madness or
imposture.

Anyone who says the gifts died with the apostles is on
very shaky ground. This theory sprang up to explain away a
much later absence of the gifts. It flies in the face of the
historical evidence.

We saw earlier that giving Christians special status if they
have a particular gift is a divisive distortion. It would make
second class Christians out of Calvin and Luther, Billy
Graham and Mother Theresa. In the same way, if all the
genuine gifts died with the apostles, we would have to
reject outright the witness and experience of Justin and
Irenaeus, Melito and Augustine and all the others. That
must mean treating them, in turn, as second class Christians.

What about all those who claim spiritual gifts today?
They are far too many to count, but include Michael Green,
John Wimber, Jim Glennon and Anne Watson. The best
you could say is that their gifts are delusions. At worst
you would have to say that their gifts were demonic
counterfeits.

John Owen, back in the seventeenth century, had a far
more balanced view than that. He didn't think the spiritual
gifts were available for his own generation, but by no means
ruled them out for the future: "It is not unlikely but that
God might on some occasions for a longer season put forth
his power in some miraculous operations, and so he may yet
do and perhaps doth sometimes." (*Pneumatologia*)

The gifts did not die with the apostles. This popular
excuse for avoiding the Spirit simply won't wash. The
evidence will not allow us to hide behind this excuse any
more. The gifts were still being enjoyed by the church many
decades after the apostles had died. Those same gifts are
being poured out by the same Holy Spirit on the Church
today.

Excuse two: The gifts are too risky

The New Testament writers insist that churches must test spiritual gifts. Their proper use cannot be taken for granted. It is possible to imitate them, whether to impress or mislead. Jonathan Edwards wrote: ". . . a work of God without stumbling blocks is never to be expected. God gives the genuine gifts. Imitations are either man-made or demonic". We have to recognise that many religious groups and cults have their own forms of prophecy and tongues, and even gifts of healing.

The gifts do become risky where there is not proper leadership. No one should try to usurp leadership because they happen to exercise an impressive gift. Excitability or a domineering attitude are no substitutes for the Spirit's still, small voice of calm.

Leaders need to work closely together and to be open to the Spirit's prompting. They need a thorough grasp of Scripture to test any word of prophecy. The gift of discernment needs to be developed and trained.

Above all, leaders need to be filled with the love of God. First, so that their love for the fellowship gives them the courage to speak out if a "gift" is not from God. Second, so that they give correction in a way that will build up and reassure any who make mistakes, and never crush them.

I remember a prayer meeting when someone prayed in a harsh and disturbing tongue. An elder leading the meeting advised that it was not from the Lord. On another occasion someone tried to whip up emotion with a long, excitable and repetitive prayer. When he stopped an elder gently but firmly commented, "You've tried to force the church to go in your direction, now please sit down and we'll wait for the Spirit to guide us together."

We must not over-react. It would be quite irresponsible to dismiss the biblical need to test spiritual gifts. But no good is achieved by overstating the risks and avoiding the gifts altogether. Some cults talk about "love-bombing" potential converts to win them over. But that is hardly a reason to abandon the New Testament vision of genuine, costly love for others.

Perhaps the most abused gift is preaching. All kinds of strange people have preached all kinds of strange messages. That doesn't mean we abandon preaching. It means that when we preach we are all the more determined to guard and proclaim the unchanging gospel of salvation.

Jesus healed. He didn't stop using the gift because some tricksters were pretending they could do it too. He didn't refuse to heal unless people promised they had never tried another healer. He didn't ask them to sign first on a dotted line that they would guarantee not to give him any bad publicity.

Jesus knew the problems. He knew all about people's mixed motives. But the gift had been given to express God's love for us. And so Jesus still healed.

In the same way, the Spirit still gives his gifts. They need testing, and he encourages that. The best way to guard them from abuse is not to lock them away, far out of reach, in a dark corner. We guard them best by putting them into action, including the gift of discernment.

John Owen summed up the attractiveness of the early Christians: "And I had rather have the order, rule, Spirit, and practice of those churches which were planted by the apostles, with all their troubles and disadvantages, than the carnal peace of others in their open degeneracy from all these things" (*Pneumatologia* quoted in Packer, *Keep in Step with the Spirit*, Leicester 1984).

If the risk were too big, God would never have given the gifts. It seems to me much more risky to use this popular excuse to justify our fear or suspicion of God's gifts. That way we risk not only rejecting the gifts, but also the giver.

Excuse three: We don't need prophecy any more

The two gifts most often rejected through popular excuses are prophecy and tongues. We need to look briefly at each of them.

Two prophecies in the book of Acts show how important the gift was. In chapter eleven, Agabus, a Christian prophet from Jerusalem, foretold a severe famine over the entire Roman world. Without waiting for disaster to strike, the Christians at Antioch immediately provided aid for the poorer churches of Judea. Two chapters later, Paul and Barnabas started their church-planting travels in obedience to prophecy: "While they were worshipping the Lord and fasting, the Holy Spirit said, 'Set apart for me Barnabas and Saul for the work to which I have called them'" (Acts 13:2).

Prophecy had quite an impact in the early church. It didn't lose its importance quickly. In AD 70 the Romans decided Jerusalem had been the centre of quite enough trouble for the Empire. They set fire to the Temple, massacred many Jews and destroyed almost the entire city. Amazingly, the Christians had advance warning of this disaster. They obeyed a command given through prophecy to pack their bags and move from the city before the trouble began:

> . . . the members of the Jerusalem Church, by means of an oracle given by revelation to acceptable persons there, were ordered to leave the city before the war began and settle in a town in Peraea called Pella. To Pella those who believed in Christ migrated from Jerusalem (Eusebius *History of the Church* 3:5).

Many modern Christians would not dream that such a warning was possible. If many churches today did receive such a warning, I doubt they would consider for a moment actually packing their bags and moving.

Not every experience of prophecy was good. Strange ideas were sometimes put round which claimed the authority of prophecy. Some Christians at Thessalonica had given up their jobs to wait eagerly for the Second Coming: someone had told them it was going to happen in just a few days or weeks.

Paul wrote quickly to put right this teaching. But he was also anxious that they wouldn't miss out on genuine prophecy in the future. Rejecting all prophecy out of hand is just as foolish as drinking in someone's words without testing them.

Paul explained to the Thessalonians how to make the most of prophecy. First, they must make sure they never treat prophecy "with contempt". Second, they need to "test everything", because only in that way can they be sure to "hold on to the good" (1 Thess 5:20–1).

The Spirit doesn't mind you testing prophecy. He wants you to. He's the one who gives the gift of discernment to sort out real prophecy from poor imitations. The Spirit is at work within us to help us test out his gifts.

There are two essential tests for any prophecy:

1 Is it in line with Scripture?
2 Does it glorify Jesus as Lord?
Two more tests can then be added:
3 What is the credibility of the prophet's daily life?
(The New Testament teaches that home life is an acid test for being able to take on public ministry.)
4 Does it feel right?
(Feelings should only be applied last. It is no good something feeling right if it contradicts Scripture or distracts from Christ. A well-intentioned effort can be thoroughly orthodox, but quite lifeless or inappropriate. They are not the qualities of a genuine word from the Lord.)
The fifth test, where any foretelling is involved, is whether it comes true (Jer 29:9).

Two more tests were added by the early church. These suggest they came across a few scoundrels and fakes. Prophets often had a travelling ministry, and were to be given hospitality by the local church. A fraud might decide he deserved bigger meals or more money:

No prophet speaking in the Spirit who orders a table spread will eat from it unless he is a false prophet (*Didache*).

The man who only imagines he has the Spirit . . . accepts payment for his prophesying, and if he does not get it he does not prophesy. It is impossible for a prophet of God to act like this (*Shepherd of Hermas*).

There's a simple test to use during a prayer meeting if you think words of prophecy are forming inside. Ask God to guide you by having a particular person pray next.

I know a girl who did this and John, the person she named, did pray next. She still wasn't convinced, and explained to God that John often prayed aloud, so could God confirm his guidance by having John pray again! God arranged things as requested, the prophecy was finally given, and a new ministry began.

The prophecy will still need testing by the fellowship, so don't claim your answered prayer makes you infallible. But if you pray like this, God will make it easier for you either to take the plunge and speak out, or to keep quiet until you really have something useful to say.

Anything done in public worship needs careful control. To many people, whatever is said at the front of a church is more or less infallible. Without public testing of any prophecy by the leaders of the church, some of the less well-informed members may be at the mercy of anything that is said. What's more, some cynics who only want to judge renewal in its worst light would then have grounds to say that a so-called prophecy was offered and no one seemed to notice or worry that it was unbiblical.

I remember one church where the minister used the apostles' creed one Sunday. It wasn't usually included in their services, and Jim got hot under the collar: he didn't like that sort of traditionalism at all, and expressed his disapproval in the form of a "prophecy". It didn't take long for the elders to realise that thus might say Jim, who thinks the Spirit has only spoken in his own lifetime. But there was no good, biblical reason at all for the Spirit of God to speak in that way.

I remember another occasion when a "prophecy" ticked off the fellowship for half-heartedness. So far so good. But then it gave dire warnings of a severe judgment, held back until now like flood waters behind a dam. God's patience had run out, the dam was about to burst, and waters of judgment would be unleashed upon the fellowship with terrible consequences.

The opening words were both biblical and relevant, but by the end there was no room left for the God who doesn't snuff out a flickering candle nor break a bruised reed. No condemnation for those who are in Christ seemed completely forgotten.

One of the elders thought this was so obviously wrong that nothing more need be said. Fortunately the others disagreed. False prophecy which contradicts the gospel of grace must gently but firmly be weeded out.

The style of prophecy has to leave itself open to these tests. It is a bit difficult to weigh a word that begins: "Thus says the Lord." I don't think any of the recorded prophecies of the New Testament period begin with this phrase. When the Old Testament prophets used it, they didn't feel obliged to put it in front of every single prophecy.

Jeremiah gave some very stern warnings about using this kind of phrase casually (chapter 23). Prophets are dressing up their own ideas as words from the Lord (Jer 23: 28). Every time a prophet has a dream he retells it as a guaranteed divine revelation (Jer 23:28). They "wag their own tongues", but have the arrogance to keep on saying "the LORD declares" (Jer 23:31). Israel glibly distorts and cheapens the "words of the living God" (Jer 23:36). When everyone dresses up their own thoughts in grand language, "every man's word becomes his own oracle" (Jer 23:26).

Jeremiah would much rather true prophets avoided this sort of phrase (Jer 23:36). God will punish those who say lightly "thus says the LORD" (Jer 23:35). He will bring everlasting shame upon those people and also upon their households (Jer 23:25, 40).

Genuine prophecy doesn't need to be dressed up in fancy language. Nor does it need to sound as if it came out of Elizabethan England, in the archaic style of the Authorised Version. It is the content of true prophecy, safeguarded by biblical tests, that makes you sit up and take notice.

A friend of mine was sitting in a prayer meeting when a prophecy was given. It was precisely directed to his personal needs about which no one else knew. When God was so unmistakably speaking to him, he only just managed to stop himself instinctively standing in God's presence.

Paul taught that prophecy is a greater gift than tongues (1 Cor 14:5). It is an outstanding gift for building up the fellowship (1 Cor 14:4), and can also have a powerful evangelistic impact, even causing an outsider to "fall down and worship God, exclaiming, 'God is really among you!'" (1 Cor 14:25).

Two or three prophets at most should speak in any one meeting (1 Cor 14:29). They can all speak in turn on different occasions (1 Cor 14:31) and all need to deliver their prophecies in a normal voice. This order and normality make it quite clear that Christian prophets do not go into some kind of pagan trance. Christians retain self-control as they prophesy, and don't become like ventriloquists' dummies (1 Cor 14:32).

Paul explained that the thread of a single prophecy can pass from one person to another. If this happens, Paul advises the first to sit down, and let the next continue (1 Cor 14:30).

In one church, a prayer meeting was enriched with this kind of prophecy which then seemed to carry on too long. The leader of the meeting prayed silently that if the words were no longer from God he would dry them up. That's what happened, and the prophets were able to learn to stop when the Spirit stops.

You may think that some rambling sermons could do

with the same treatment. I'm afraid I haven't heard of the same prayer being equally effective when directed at a pulpit!

Paul said he would like every Christian to pray in tongues. He would like even more for every Christian to prophesy (1 Cor 14:5). He begins 1 Corinthians 14 by encouraging Christians to desire eagerly the spiritual gifts, especially prophecy (v. 1). To make it quite clear where he stands, he ends the chapter on the same theme: "Therefore my brothers, *be eager to prophesy*, and do not forbid speaking in tongues. But everything should be done in a fitting and orderly way" (1 Cor 14:39–40).

Paul is in good company, for Moses valued prophecy just as highly. But in Moses' day, the Spirit was not yet poured out on all believers: "But Moses replied, '. . . *I wish that all the LORD's people were prophets*, and that the LORD would put his Spirit on them!'" (Num 11:29).

In all that the New Testament says, there is absolutely no indication that prophecy won't be needed any more when the New Testament writings are complete. True prophecy does not claim for itself the same status as Scripture, and certainly never pretends to replace Scripture. In the experience of many Christians the gift of prophecy doesn't distract from Scripture. Instead, it enhances the Bible's supreme authority.

Prophecy is much more than foretelling. It is more often a word of comfort, rebuke or guidance, addressed to the immediate needs of a particular fellowship or individual. In general it is best not to write down and pass round prophecies. They are given for particular occasions, not for all time, and usually have one-off relevance. We don't have a record of most of the prophecies which were given to the churches of New Testament times.

Prophecy is subordinate to Scripture, and is given by God to complement Scripture, just as he helps with the words of new hymns and songs and guides a preacher. According to the New Testament, it is a most valuable gift, which can greatly enrich the life of a local fellowship.

Faced with all the clear teaching and promises of the New Testament, we surely need prophecy in the Church today. We need it now as much as it has ever been needed in the past. We must learn to hear afresh Paul's command that we should eagerly desire the very special gift of prophecy.

Excuse four: What's the use of speaking in tongues?

The gift of tongues had me puzzled. Some only mentioned it in suspicious or dismissive tones. They preferred not to speak of it at all. Others talked about it non stop. Some of those who were high on tongues used it like spiritual valium. Neither group seemed very helpful. In the New Testament, speaking in tongues is neither rejected out of hand nor treated as the bees' knees of spiritual gifts and the answer to your every problem.

I could see the problem of emotionalism — putting feelings before the promise of new life in Christ. That made the truth of the Bible less decisive for faith than which side I got out of bed each day. It really wouldn't do. But I confused any emotion with excessive emotion, and thought tongues always made people into emotion-addicts.

Then I met misuse of the gift. Paul said "two — or at the most three should speak," one at a time (1 Cor 14:27). He added that interpretation is a *must* (1 Cor 14:27). He even discouraged the gift's use when unbelievers are present, in case they think the Christians are "out of their minds" (1 Cor 14:22-3). All of this makes it quite clear that tongues is under the control of the tongues-speaker. It is never frenzied or ecstatic babbling, on "automatic pilot."

The New Testament is quite clear that any spiritual gift can be misused. Thomas Hardy wrote a poem called "In Church" which describes a successful preacher. After the service the door to his vestry blew open, and there he was "with a satisfied smile" rerunning his sermon in dumb show before a mirror. He misused his gift and discredited it before his congregation. But the wrong lay not in the gift but in the heart of its user.

My first encounter with tongues was unhelpful. The speakers seemed frightened and frenzied. My reaction was to write off tongues as a meaningless practice. My judgment was shallow, like finding one cracked egg in my weekly shopping and deciding never to buy anything from a supermarket again.

If you reject a gift, you reject the giver. If you reject a particular kind of Christian, you reject Christ in them. My problem was serious. I accepted in theory that God gave the gift. But my heart was set against it.

Many people request the gift of tongues to enrich their prayer-life. I had to pray for tongues too, but for a very different reason. My gut reaction was so opposed to this gift, it was only praying specifically for it that I could be delivered from my prejudice. Only by this uncomfortable prayer could I stop quenching the Spirit and be put right with God.

That was ten years ago. The gift didn't come dramatically, but it came in time. Now it has special value for me.

First it is a love language. Some couples have private ways of talking together. They make up special phrases which mean a lot to them. But they would be meaningless or plain silly to anyone else. Tongues can give that kind of intimacy to prayer. Praise is lifted above enthusiastic thanksgiving into adoration and love. God's presence becomes more real.

Second, it comes into its own when ordinary words fail. I remember meeting an old friend on a train. It soon became clear that he had drifted away from God, but we couldn't go into detail before the train reached my station. I'd only glimpsed the problem, and didn't know when I'd see him again. I felt an urgent need to pray, but what could I say? Instinctively I prayed in tongues, and felt caught up into the great eternal prayer of Jesus — "at the right hand of God and interceding for us" (Rom 8:4).

Words don't just fail when praying for others. An unkind joke can bite deeper than ever intended. Once in particular I felt cut to the raw. The comment probably wasn't meant that way, and showing my reaction wouldn't have helped.

On my way home I prayed in tongues, expressing a pain deeper than words could say. God helped me to tell him about the hurt and then he moved me beyond it. I found I was praying not for myself but for the one who hurt me. As I did so I received a new love for them. Left to myself, I would probably have held on to my hurt, and become angry or resentful. Praying in tongues delivered me from my pain and drew me into God's love.

Before preaching and counselling I often pray in tongues. I find it invaluable. Tongues enriches my openness to God. It makes me more available to receive his power. Paul talks of the Spirit leading us in prayer "too deep for words" (Rom 8:26). I would by no means say that tongues is essential for this, or that tongues is the only way. But for me, at least, these are the practical values and uses of the gift.

All good gifts bring risks and temptations. Tongues is no different. For me, the three main risks are legalism, self-indulgence and false superiority.

Legalism is when I feel that praying in tongues is strictly necessary to receive power. Then it becomes a skill under my control, rather than an undeserved gift from God. Tongues is not superstitious, as if a day without it is a day of disaster. Tongues does not have automatic results, as if it was a 999 call on a celestial hot-line.

Self-indulgence is when the sheer pleasure of praying in tongues threatens to squeeze out prayer in English. Some people have this problem with songs of worship: they can end up taking all the time available for prayer. Some are tempted to spend all their time praying about themselves. Others have an ever-growing shopping list of requests for others. Too much time on any one type of prayer distorts our whole relationship with God.

Tongues complements other kinds of prayer, but it should never replace them. Paul said he prayed in tongues more than any of the Corinthians (1 Cor 14:18). But he also wrote down many magnificent prayers in his everyday Greek.

If you want to understand the New Testament's teaching on tongues, you need to study I Corinthians 14. There Paul stresses the value of the gift and the best ways to use it in a local fellowship.

False superiority always tries to elbow its way in. Paul insists that spiritual gifts are *never* a reward for what we have done. They are God's gift of undeserved love to his Church. Paul suggests that tongues is a common gift. He'd like everyone to receive it (1 Cor 14:5). But he *never* suggests it is vital for true discipleship.

Paul makes it clear that tongues is a genuine gift of the Spirit. It shouldn't be forbidden, because all God's gifts are good (1 Cor 14:39). Christians should never presume to pick and choose among the spiritual gifts according to their own taste. But Paul *never* recommends tongues as a sort of charismatic aspirin or cure-all, to be taken three times a day whatever a particular Christian's need or problem.

Praying in tongues is also called "praying with my spirit," and normal prayer is "praying with my mind" (1 Cor 14:14). Paul says both are valuable. He also speaks of "singing with my spirit" and "singing with my mind" (1 Cor 14:15).

In the early church, singing in the Spirit developed out of the practice of "jubilation" — spontaneous, improvised elaboration upon the word "Alleluia." Augustine called this "singing on vowel sounds." Pope Gregory said it arose "when we conceive such great joy in the heart that we cannot express it in words." Any who have heard the exquisitely beautiful harmonies of such singing will know why this can often seem a most glorious foretaste of the worship of heaven.

Once I couldn't understand the gift of tongues, and so I didn't want it. Now I wouldn't be without it. For me it is a source of great encouragement. But it is not the be-all and end-all of Christian living. God chooses who receives each gift, and God knows best. So don't look down on those who don't have your particular gift. And don't be resentful that God doesn't always give us our "first choice" gift. He really does know best.

If you know the inspiration of the gift of tongues, remember that God the Spirit gives many other gifts, guides and instructs, convicts of sin and desires to fulfil the Great Commission through us.

If you are hostile in your heart towards tongues or any other New Testament gift, you need to pray that through with God. I hope my experience may be useful to you. If you reject a particular gift, you are rejecting the giver of them all. And that's very serious.

Reasons or excuses?

Most of the objections we have looked at have some value in correcting an unhealthy, unbiblical overstatement. But reasons often turn into excuses. We hide behind other people's mistakes to try to avoid the Spirit. That means quenching the Spirit within us, and shutting out any deeper experience of his presence.

Jesus didn't call us to have one hundred and one reasons why Anglicans or Methodists or whoever have got it all correct. He called us to follow him. If I have the most carefully worked out theology of the Spirit, and use it to avoid his fullness, my theology is worthless. It has become an evasion, a barricade for my sinfulness, for my self-sufficiency and for my fear. It is, in reality, no more than an excuse.

The popular excuses for avoiding the Spirit won't wash. They are a cover-up for the fact that we want to keep control of our own lives. We prefer to keep a firm grip on how much real influence we will hand over to God.

The two most popular excuses are often at loggerheads. One person says, "I received the Spirit at conversion, let's change the subject." Another says, "I received the Spirit at a particular experience, let me tell you about it." Both risk saying "I've got it all." Both risk living in the past.

Jesus doesn't want us to "get more of it" but to give more of ourselves to his Spirit. He doesn't want us to live in the past, but to keep in step with the Spirit *today* (Gal 5:25).

The message of the New Testament is plain. Give up your excuses for avoiding the Spirit. Know the Spirit's presence, with you and within you. And go on, day by day, being filled afresh with the life-giving, life-transforming Spirit of the living God.

Part Four

GROWING IN THE SPIRIT

GO ON BEING FILLED

Home is where you relax. You feel accepted for who you are. There's nothing to prove to anyone, and you don't have to be constantly on your best behaviour. You can be yourself, and put your feet up.

You soon know if you're not at home with someone. Conversation becomes difficult. You begin to perch awkwardly on the edge of a chair. It can be your own house, but some people make you feel no longer at home.

One day soon after we moved to Bromley, there was a knock at the front door. I opened it, and to my surprise I was faced with a policewoman, who asked if she could come in for a few minutes.

My mind raced as I invited her into the lounge. Had I been speeding or had I driven through a red light? Could I have committed some major offence without knowing it? I felt thoroughly guilty, but tried not to act as if caught red-handed. Every step to the lounge was one more step of the sentenced prisoner towards the condemned cell.

As we sat down, I braced myself to hear that anything I said might be taken down and used in evidence against me. After what seemed an eternity, the clouds cleared. She was a friend of the people who used to own the house, and simply wanted their new address.

One thing was certain. Until I found out why she was there, I was certainly not at home, even though we had so recently bought the house. I think she rather enjoyed my few moments of innocent discomfort!

We usually think of God as "up there" and "out there". He reigns on high, and that can often seem far away from our everyday world. If we are not very careful, prayer becomes like a very long distance telephone call with a poor line. We talk about prayers "hitting the ceiling" if our relationship with God turns dry for a while. It's as if the prayers that "get through" pass beyond the ceiling and through the atmosphere, finally reaching God "up there" and "out there".

This way of thinking also confines God to special places. We begin to feel God is only present in religious buildings – the houses of God. Then it helps if they have an old-fashioned, medieval feel about them. When Liverpool Cathedral was built in traditional Gothic style, one national newspaper commented that God prefers Gothic.

A friend of ours belongs to a church whose building is very modern. When outsiders come to sample it, in case they want to be married there, some have been heard to say: "It's really not suitable at all. We want to get married in a proper church!"

Jesus' teaching about the Spirit is very different to this "up there" and "out there" way of thinking. His promise of the Spirit broke new ground in four decisive ways:

1 The Spirit comes forever (John 14:16)
We no longer receive temporary inspiration like Old Testament prophets and heroes. We don't even enjoy a special intervention by God for a limited period, like the three year ministry of Jesus. Instead, in every generation and in every part of the world, Jesus promised the permanent presence of God's Spirit.

2 The Spirit is with us (John 14:17)
The Spirit doesn't live in buildings made of bricks and mortar. He cannot be trapped or contained in church buildings, or locked up safely with the church silver. The gift of the Spirit isn't for Sundays and special religious occasions only. He is God with us.

3 The Spirit is within us (John 14:16)
This may sound familiar. Many Christians are used to

the *idea* of the "indwelling" of the Spirit. But long words can kill life. The breakthrough comes when we make it practical and personal. God lives in me.

Put as bluntly as this, it would seem blasphemous if Jesus hadn't said it. It can help a great deal to stop three times each day for a week simply to pray: "Thank you God. It really is true. Your Spirit lives in me."

Simple truths often take a long time to sink in. But once "God inside me" begins to register, the practical impact can be dynamite!

4 At home with God (John 14:23)
Jesus still hadn't finished his radical new teaching about the permanent presence of the Spirit. A few verses later he gave this remarkable promise:

"If anyone loves me, he will obey my teaching. My Father will love him, and we will come to him and make our home with him" (John 14:23).

Jesus put it as plainly as possible – "we will come to him." Christians can give up those old ideas about a far away God, "up there" and "out there". He doesn't "come down to be with us" only when we meet for worship. The Holy Trinity is right here with us all the time.

God is not just with us and within us. Jesus claimed that God will make his home with us. This is not said lightly. It does not diminish the awe-inspiring holiness, majesty and power of God. On Jesus' lips these words do not domesticate God, reducing him to the status of a pagan household god.

The promise of Jesus stands. In the new age of the Spirit, God has made his home with us. Because there is no condemnation for those born again in Christ, and because the Spirit is within us and encourages us to call God "Abba", Jesus told us we can be "at home" with God.

Jesus promised we can be at home with God at all times, in our own houses, in our daily routine, and wherever we go. Jesus' own life showed this in action. Paul confirmed this was the experience of the first Christians: "God has poured out his love into our hearts by the Holy Spirit, whom he has given us" (Rom 5:5). As we rediscover the Spirit, we reclaim our glorious inheritance in Christ. As we rediscover the Spirit, we can rediscover being at home with God. We need not think of God only being "up there" and "out there" ever again.

The Spirit of discipleship

Discipleship concerns the whole of life. The freedom to be at home with God is not specially reserved for Sundays. To be filled with the Spirit means to bring the whole of life under Christ's active Lordship, as we are changed to be more like him.

Home is where your heart is. But Jesus said your heart is where your treasure is (Matt 6:21). We cannot be fully at home with God if the things that really matter most, and set the basic shape of our lives, are centred on this world's priorities. It won't help us much if in theory we rediscover

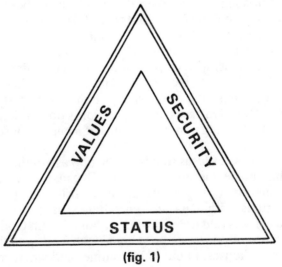

(fig. 1)

the Spirit, but in practice we are still banking on treasure on earth (Matt 6:20–1).

If someone asked where our heart is, or whether we are putting our hearts into discipleship, we might say in the words of the old song that our heart now belongs to Jesus. But Jesus claims the right to probe us more deeply. More than anywhere else he does this in the Sermon on the Mount.

In Matthew chapter 6, Jesus reveals how three things come together to form a triangle: values, security and status. Jesus describes the triangle within which we usually live, and at the same time he shows us a better way. (fig. 1)

1 Values

What matters most in your life? What do you really want out of life? What are your greatest dreams for your future? The real test of our values is not our profession of faith. The values that shape us are the things that fill our minds and dominate our thoughts.

What do you think about when you can't sleep? Jesus has a pretty good idea: "So do not worry, saying, 'What shall we eat?' or 'What shall we drink?' or 'What shall we wear?'" (Matt 6:31). We can give worldly values the slogan *More is best*.

2 Security

Where is your security rooted? Our main security can often be our job. Many people suffer acute problems of depression faced with redundancy or retirement. Security also involves the group of people where we belong most.

We can sum up security in terms of income, career, and social circle, and also for many people, family and patriotic pride. The problem is not having these things. It's letting them tell us how to live. Jesus put his finger on the problem: "No one can serve two masters. Either he will hate the one and love the other, or he will be devoted to the one and despise the other. You cannot serve both God and Money" (Matt 6:24). Our slogan is: *My place in society*.

216

3 Status

What gives you your identity? What makes you the person you are? If someone asks, "What are you?", they usually expect an answer in terms of a job. In business you ask, "Is he important?" Back comes the reply, "He's worth so many thousand a year."

It has often been said that the poor are not "important" enough to hurt the pockets of the rich. The two-thirds world are not a major election issue in the rich countries.

James described an early church where if a visitor was wealthy, he would be given one of the best seats. But if a poor man dropped in, he would be left standing at the back, or invited to sit on the floor (Jas 2:1–4). Status decides who we are prepared to sit next to, or who we invite to our homes.

In job and background, in education and sporting ability, our worth is often assessed competitively. That means we have to keep on proving ourselves to maintain our status and preserve our self-image.

I remember a TV programme about a Swiss finishing school. One girl had just failed an exam, and phoned her father with the bad news. She said something like this: "Sorry I didn't make it this time, Daddy. One day I'll do something to earn your love." Parental love was apparently on probation: she felt she wouldn't be genuinely loved until her success deserved it.

Jesus dealt with our status: "Look at the birds of the air; they do not sow or reap or store away in barns, and yet your heavenly Father feeds them. Are you not much more valuable than they?" (Matt 6:26). Our slogan for status is: *Better than you.*

The triangle of this world

Some of the attitudes I have mentioned are not wrong in themselves. But the slogans are. They come together to form an almost impregnable triangle of social conformity. Jesus didn't call us to a spiritual hobby. He called us to a way of life. Much of the time, we are genuinely committed Christians in our private lives, but caught in the triangle of materialism: (fig. 2)

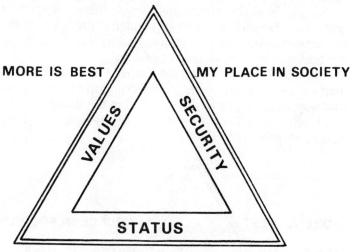

BETTER THAN YOU
(fig. 2)

The triangle imprisons our faith and controls our basic loyalty. If we try to live as Christians inside it we feel trapped, we feel frustrated, and we secretly know our lives are self-contradictory.

We don't belong in the triangle of the world any more. But we can't find a way to escape. We seem locked in to our old, instinctive values, security and status.

Jesus talked about moths, rust and thieves. Today we can add built-in obsolescence. When we store up treasure on earth, Jesus warned we are being no different to anyone else: "The pagans run after these things" (Matt 6:32). Jesus made it quite clear he was calling all who want to follow him not just to a new set of beliefs, but to a new life of discipleship. He didn't have in mind ordinary respectable living within the triangle of the world: "If you love those who love you, what reward will you get? Are not even the tax collectors doing that? And if you greet only your brothers, *what are you doing more than others?"* (Matt 5:46–7).

We are, in Jesus' terms, investing a life in things that don't last. He didn't tell us to condemn us. Satan is the condemner, who wants to crush us under guilt. Jesus raised our horizons in order to deliver us.

All Jesus' teaching about the Father's love can be summed up in this phrase: your life is too important to waste in that way. Jesus wants to deliver us from the triangle of the world. See how Jesus' words are set against our three normal slogans: (fig. 3)

MORE IS BEST

Do not worry
(Matt 6:31)

MY PLACE IN SOCIETY

No one can serve
two masters
(Matt 6:24)

VALUES

SECURITY

STATUS

BETTER THAN YOU
Your Heavenly Father
(Matt 6:26,32)

(fig. 3)

Jim Wallis recognised just how important these words of Jesus are:

If in fact most Christians are more rooted in the principalities of this world than they are in the local community of faith, it is no wonder the church is in trouble. Clearly, the social reality in which we feel most rooted will be the one that will determine . . . the way we live. It is not enough to talk of Christian fellowship while our security is based elsewhere. We will continue to conform to the values and institutions of our society as long as our security is grounded in them (*Call to Conversion*, Tring 1982).

The triangle of Jesus

Jesus' teaching confronts the world's triangle. So does his life. When Jesus said, "Seek first the Kingdom of God and his righteousness" (Matt 6:33), he described the way he was already living.

1 Values

Jesus did his father's business. He loved people as individuals, regardless of personal cost. The love of money and possessions never clouded his priorities. He replaced "More is best" with *the Kingdom of God*.

2 Security

Jesus outraged the Temple authorities. He got into trouble for not being religious enough. For his last three years he had no real home, and no bed he could always call his own. "Foxes have holes and birds of the air have nests, but the Son of Man has no place to lay his head" (Matt 8:20).

With his disciples he developed a new bond of brotherly love and belonging. He said all who chose to follow him were his brothers and sisters. In the twelve who travelled with Jesus were the beginnings of the Church, not as a religious institution, but as the new community of love. Jesus replaced "My place in society" with *the Family of God*.

3 Status

Jesus came from an ordinary working family. He didn't have a university education or special training at a theological college. He mixed with common people, and was often found with the down-and-outs and the social outcasts – leprosy sufferers, the Empire's taxmen, and prostitutes. They were the people you were meant to avoid if you wanted a reputation for being holy and religious.

Jesus was unemployed. He had little social status and no career prospects. But he had an uncanny confidence in God's love, guidance and power. He replaced "Better than you" with *Son of God*.

Jesus' life and teaching fit together perfectly. You can see this at a glance if we look at Jesus' triangle together with his three key words of advice. (fig. 4)

The first Christians dared to be different. It was never easy, but they took seriously Jesus' teaching. They worked hard at switching from the world's to Jesus' triangle. We can illustrate this very briefly from theory in Ephesians and from practice in Acts.

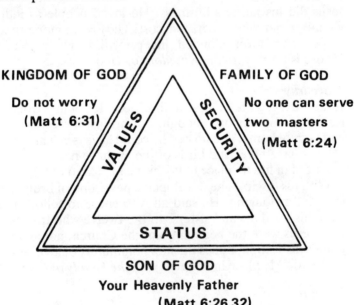

(fig. 4)

1 Values – The Kingdom of God
Eph 4:22–4   You were taught, with regard to your former way of life, to put off your old self, which is being corrupted by its deceitful desires; to be made new in the attitude of your minds; and to put on the new self, created to be like God in true righteousness and holiness.
Acts 4:34   There were no needy persons among them . . . money was distributed to anyone as he had need.

2 Security – The Family of God
Eph 4:2, 32   Be completely humble and gentle; be patient, bearing with one another in love . . . Be kind and compassionate to one another, forgiving each other, just as in Christ God forgave you.
Acts 2:42   They devoted themselves to the apostles' teaching and to the fellowship, to the breaking of bread and to prayer.

3 Status – The Children of God
Eph 4:4–6   There is one body and one Spirit – just as you were called to one hope when you were called – one Lord, one faith, one baptism; one God and Father of all, who is over all and through all and in all.
Acts 2:46–7 They broke bread in their homes and ate together with glad and sincere hearts, praising God.

We are faced with a stark choice: Jesus' triangle or the world's triangle? Do we dare to be different, like the first disciples? Or do we continue to live in frustrated self-contradiction?

Jesus didn't ever say it would be easy. But he did say, "Follow me." As isolated Christians, the pressure to conform to the world's priorities is often overwhelming. We can only go so far in following Jesus before we feel terribly exposed.

Only together can we have the strength to resist and to begin to live a more obviously different way to our neighbours. Only together can we break the triangle of the world. That's not surprising. Jesus calls us to follow him, not merely as individual Christians, but as the new community of the Spirit.

The house on the rock

The last part of the Sermon on the Mount is one of Jesus' most familiar parables: the wise and foolish men building on the rock and the sand (Matt 7:24–7). We are used to the idea that Christ is the solid rock of salvation.

> On Christ the solid rock I stand
> All other ground is shifting sand

In verse 24 Jesus draws a different point from the parable. These words are very important, because they refer back to the teaching of the whole sermon: "Everyone who hears these words of mine *and puts them into practice* is like a wise man who built his house on the rock."

Only when born again can we begin to do this. It's no good trying to live like Jesus in our own strength. We are bound to run out of steam fast. Only when we receive the Spirit of holiness can we begin to live like Jesus.

Paul's model for the new way of living was Christ. The practical instructions in his letters always echo the Sermon on the Mount. He eagerly wanted Christians to break out from the triangle of the world. "Don't let the world squeeze you into its mould, but be transformed" (Rom 12:2).

We have seen that a genuine Christian, locked into the world's triangle struggles with a frustrating, self-contradictory life. But Paul said it was no longer he who lived, but Christ within (Gal 2:20). An early Christian called Jerome wrote, "He is rich enough who is poor in Christ."

Jesus urged us as strongly as he could to break out of that worldly triangle. He invited us to build on the rock by putting his teaching and his example into practice. He called us to seek first the Kingdom of God, and to let Jesus' own triangle shape our life together.

We are not called to take up our cross daily within the world's triangle. We are called to take up our cross and follow Jesus. The Spirit of discipleship is the Spirit of deliverance from this world's priorities. Only as we rediscover the Spirit can we "put it into practice" in Jesus' triangle. (fig. 5)

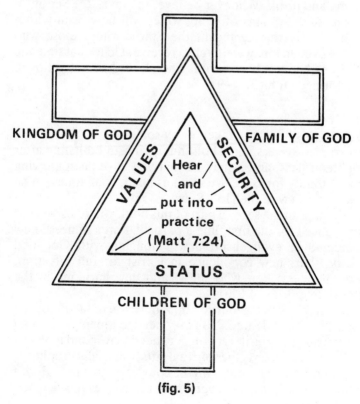

KINGDOM OF GOD   VALUES   Hear and put into practice (Matt 7:24)   SECURITY   FAMILY OF GOD

STATUS

CHILDREN OF GOD

(fig. 5)

God's living waters

At the end of this chapter I want to turn to one more promise of Jesus. More than any other, this is the clear invitation of the Man of the Spirit who is also the Lord of the Spirit to drink deeply and to carry on drinking God's life-giving waters. We are considering this after looking at Jesus' call to costly discipleship, because being filled with the Spirit is always life-changing, and never just an isolated experience for its own sake.

> On the last and greatest day of the Feast, Jesus stood and said in a loud voice, "If a man is thirsty, let him come to me and drink. Whoever believes in me, as the Scripture has said, streams of living water will flow from within him." By this he meant the Spirit, whom those who believed in him were later to receive. Up to that time the Spirit had not been given, since Jesus had not yet been glorified (John 7:37–9).

1 If you thirst

I hope this book has taken away some of your fear of the unknown. Jesus spoke about hungering and thirsting after righteousness, and it may be that you have been growing more thirsty for God. We all of us need, at all times, to be filled afresh with the Holy Spirit.

Perhaps in the second part of this book you rediscovered or realised for the first time a particular area of need: new boldness in evangelism; new belonging with God and each other; new confidence in Christ for full salvation; new holiness; new wholeness; and new harmony in the indivisible Body of Christ.

Or maybe your favourite popular excuse for avoiding the Spirit has been dented. You may need to repent of running away from the Spirit. Or you may need to respond to Paul's call to desire eagerly the spiritual gifts, especially prophecy.

Your thirst may centre on the conviction that though you received the Spirit at conversion, you have never welcomed him nor consciously recognised his presence. It may be that you need a moment of breakthrough, when you pass over from defective teaching to the normal New Testament experience of being filled with the Spirit. This is never just for "spiritual superstars" or for "a different sort of Christian to me".

We saw that to be filled with the Spirit is both an invitation and a command. God wants to go on filling you with his Spirit. If you are thirsty for him, now may be the moment to begin.

2 Come to me

John confirms that the Spirit was not given in the new way Jesus promised until Jesus had been glorified (John 7:39). The Spirit is always and only given through Jesus. His purpose and desire is always and only to glorify Jesus.

If you are thirsty for the Holy Spirit, come to Jesus in prayer. If you are thirsty to live closer to Jesus, to love him and know him better, then pray to him. He will answer you with the gift of his Spirit.

> Come, all you who are thirsty,
>   come to the waters;
> and you that have no money,
>   come, buy and eat!
> Come, buy wine and milk
>   without money and without cost.
> Why spend money on what is not bread,
>   and your labour on what does not satisfy?
> Listen, listen to me, and eat what is good,
>   and your soul will delight in the richest of fare.
>
> (Isa 55:1–2)

Jesus stresses that you must believe as you come. Believe his promise. Claim it for your own. And just as at conversion, thank him that his promise is being fulfilled.

3 Drink

Last week I was kept awake two nights with a swollen and

226

tender throat. I needed a large glass of water in the
bedroom to keep me going through the night. It had to sit
on a high shelf to be safely out of reach from our toddler's
early morning "explorations".

As I lay awake but sleepy, the last thing I felt like doing
was getting out of bed to pick up the glass. Unless I did, the
water was available but completely useless.

If you come to Jesus but don't drink, your thirst will
never be satisfied. The Spirit has been in you since conversion. From that moment he could have filled you, but he has
been waiting for you to drink. The first sip isn't meant to
last a lifetime.

You may have been filled in the past, but now have run
dry. Jesus invites us to drink and carry on drinking. We
need to stay open to God, and that means staying receptive
to his Spirit. Just as we always need to come back to God for
fresh forgiveness, we need to come back to him daily to be
filled and refilled with the Holy Spirit.

4 Streams of living water
Living in the Spirit means living for Christ and living for
others. The Spirit doesn't flow into our hearts for the sake
of our own feelings. He makes us into living sacrifices,
offering all that we are to God in worship that embraces the
whole of life. And as we open ourselves to God, the
life-giving Spirit increasingly flows through us into the vast
desert of human needs in our pagan world.

As we go on being filled, the Spirit keeps flowing. He
wants us to keep on giving out in worship and service. And
he wants us to keep on receiving more and more of the
inexhaustible riches of Christ. Only in that way can we
continue to become more like Christ. Paul summed up
God's plan for us:

So then, just as you received Christ Jesus as Lord,
continue to live in him, rooted and built up in him,
strengthened in the faith as you were taught, and over-
flowing with thankfulness (Col 2:6–7).

Are you thirsty for God? Come to Christ. Drink. And let God's streams of living waters flow freely through you. May I urge and encourage you to pray now to be filled anew with the Holy Spirit. Then seek to go on being filled, day by day, with the life-giving, life-transforming Spirit of the living God.